MALAI

Frozen Desserts Inspired by South Asian Flavors

POOJA BAVISHI

PHOTOGRAPHY BY MORGAN IONE YEAGER

weldon**owen**

For Ma and Dad.
You did, so I can.
. . . arre abhi toh party shuru hui hai!

CONTENTS

FOREWORD

Malai **has been one of my favorite** food words since I was a kid. It's the cream that I would steal off the top of the milk when my parents were not looking. To me, *malai* represents indulgence, decadence, and a scrumptious bite. That's exactly what Pooja Bavishi has created with Malai—and here she shares the secrets to incredible frozen desserts with South Asian flavors.

When I first tasted Malai's ice creams, I was hooked. And as a judge on Food Network's *Chopped* and other cooking shows, I've had the opportunity to taste some of the most creative dishes out there.

The release of my own cookbook, *Chaat*, is what led me to a beautiful friendship and a remarkable partnership with Pooja. I got a glimpse of her inspired, creative mind at work: while chaats are typically savory, Pooja crafted genius sweet creations like date tamarind ice cream, cilantro mint sorbet, and frozen yogurt raita. She has shown that her flavor alchemy is far ahead of so many in the industry.

Pooja has the unique talent of harnessing the beauty and vibrancy of South Asian flavors, techniques, and colors into absolutely stunning and delicious ice creams. She can conjure the most sophisticated flavors into desserts with techniques that are innovative yet still have a hint of nostalgia. Pooja's infectious smile and demeanor shine through everything she creates. Her passion for taking people on a wonderful journey makes whatever she does spectacular.

Ice cream flavors like Masala Chai, Golden Turmeric, Jaggery, and Fenugreek with Walnuts are just a few of the intriguing recipes in this book. Beyond ice creams, you'll find dairy-free frozen desserts, ice cream desserts, baked goods, toppings, and sauces. The approachability of each recipe makes this book accessible for everyone. My favorite part is the personal stories and journey that Pooja has included alongside her inspiring recipes.

This book is a visual feast, and I can't wait to churn my way through it.

Maneet Chauhan
chef and TV personality

INTRODUCTION

I love the smell of chai. To me, it's everything comforting: sweet, spiced (and spicy), and creamy. It smells like home. I often think that I developed my identity through chai. My mom would make cups of chai for herself and my dad every morning. My sister and I would get baby sips mixed with milk. But it was the real thing, in my parents' cups, that intoxicated me. Nearly every morning, I would ask to smell their chai, then stick my nose right into their cups to soak in all the milky, spiced sweetness rich with ginger, cardamom, cloves, and cinnamon—a powerful connection to a homeland that I grew up feeling nostalgic for.

I've thought a lot about why I started Malai. For years, I spoke about my dreams of eventually opening and operating a dessert business, but I could never really figure out what it would look like. The ideas kept coming, but nothing felt quite right, that is, until I started to make ice creams. It was then that some part of me instinctively knew to combine Indian flavors and spices that did not traditionally go together—rose and cinnamon, saffron and black pepper, green mango and cardamom, cayenne and star anise—but that shine through so beautifully in butterfat and dairy. For the

first time, I had a platform to express my whole self.

Malai is exactly the project I've dreamed of my whole life—one that celebrates Indian heritage and culinary traditions in a delicious way for a diverse audience. I relish being able to tell the stories of what it was like for me to embrace the Indian flavors in my suburban American upbringing. And one of my greatest sources of joy is connecting to people through these flavors.

There have been countless times when I've seen customers try Malai ice cream and recall something familiar from their own background, whether a memory of their father using fresh ingredients to make ice cream when they were children, the cooking of an Indian friend who uses similar flavors, or the fragrance of a grandmother's perfume. Unexpectedly, the flavors are somehow universal.

Coming to know that there is a market for the tastes and aromas of my childhood has demonstrated itself in many ways. At the shop, day after day, month after month, our customers tell us that Malai is the best ice cream that they've ever had—not the best Indian ice cream but the best ice

cream. Acceptance is also evident in the many collaborations we've been fortunate to put together over the years, such as our project with celebrity chef Maneet Chauhan, with whom we made a "chaat" sundae based on the iconic Indian street food, or our annual Guest Chef Series, when we invite such well-known chefs and cookbook authors as Kristen Kish, Dorie Greenspan (whose recipe makes an appearance in this book on pages 114–115), Erin Jeanne McDowell, and Jessie Sheehan to make a signature dish using our ice creams.

I know that I'm now telling the story that I've been wanting to share since I was a child, since those early days when I craved to learn about the traditions of my family while also wanting to show my heritage as not merely different but also of value and appeal to everyone. And it's not just the inspiration from my culture that I'm bringing to Malai and to this book. It is also the long list of fabulous ice cream and dessert professionals who have shaped my journey. So much of what I learned from them serves as the foundation of these recipes.

Malai may be one of the first businesses to bring these flavors and flavor combina-

jaggery is a South Asian molded sugar with a molasses-rich smokiness that you will always want to have in your pantry.

And that is exactly the reason why I also wanted to write a cookbook—an ice cream–centered book that celebrates the flavors of my childhood, that makes accessible and familiar and craveable what was once considered foreign. This book will highlight the first-generation experience as well as celebrate the bounty of beautiful ingredients and spices of my Indian background

> "Malai is exactly the project I've dreamed of my whole life—one that celebrates Indian heritage and culinary traditions in a delicious way for a diverse audience."

tions to the world of ice cream, but they have been around for generations, just as South Asians have been a part of the American landscape for generations. I have wondered why these ingredients, which some 1.5 billion people around the world eat on a daily basis, are not more widely enjoyed in this country. I want to believe that we are ready for the moment when it is as "normal" to pull a pint of masala chai ice cream from your grocery store freezer as it is a pint of cookies and cream. Let's flavor ice cream with rose water and cardamom. Let's break out the saffron for more than just a few special dishes. Let's understand that there are different types of sugar around the world and that

that are readily available to all of us in this country. And it will teach you how to make the most flavorful and creamy ice cream you have ever had. I want to change how we think about ice cream. Come join me!

PANTRY STAPLES

Pantry staples are whatever you use on a daily basis. But there are some items, while not staples, I think you should have on hand all the time, not just for special occasions. Everything I list here has multiple uses, both sweet and savory, and can be used in ice creams, baked goods, and even sprinkled atop your favorite fruit bowl. I hope that you will look to these ingredients not just for when you're making something that you typically don't prepare but also to enhance the dishes you make every day.

JAGGERY

Made from sugarcane, this unrefined South Asian sugar has heavy notes of molasses, similar in flavor to brown sugar. It is traditionally sold in block form, and you must use a knife to shave off the amount needed for a recipe, though now it is also readily available in powdered form. It has a distinctive taste with deep caramel notes and an almost creamy consistency that sets it apart from other sugars. It's a one-to-one replacement for brown sugar and adds a touch of earthiness to typical dishes.

ROSE WATER

I don't remember a life without rose water, and moving forward, you shouldn't either. I can see how rose water can be polarizing, as it can have the aura of your grandmother's perfume. But used in the right amount, it can elevate a dessert to the next level. It adds an air of sophistication and nuance to a plain ice cream or baked good. And for an extra bonus, if you already have rose water in your pantry, you can use it as a toner to smooth your skin!

CANDIED FENNEL SEEDS

This really should just be fennel seeds, but I'm doing you a favor by recommending you keep candied fennel seeds in your pantry. They're fun! They're colorful! But they also have the delicious properties of plain fennel seeds—that slight licorice note that serves as both a palate cleanser and a digestive aid. There is nothing that this little seed can't do. Candied fennel seeds will add a pop of color and flavor in place of the usual dessert-type sprinkles and are also delightful to munch on by themselves after a meal.

REALLY GOOD SPICES

Using high-quality fresh whole spices will make all the difference not only in the recipes in this book but also in anything else you make. Using ground spices that were packed into jars long ago has become the norm, but things can be different! At Malai, we purchase our spices from quality companies, such as Burlap & Barrel, Curio Spice Co., Diaspora Co., Heilala, and Heray Spice. They source what they sell ethically and provide the freshest

spices available, which, in turn, makes our products better. Invest in fresh whole spices, and they will make yours better too.

GARAM MASALA

The one pantry spice that I will call out is garam masala, a spice blend. Although its content varies from company to company, it most typically includes cinnamon, cardamom, cumin, cloves, and black peppercorns—basically a lot of warming spices with some heat. But when I came across Cardoz Legacy's garam masala, which is made of *all* warming spices—cinnamon, star anise, bay leaf, black cardamom, yellow cardamom, mace, and cloves—I was hooked. This is the garam masala I used for testing the recipes that follow, the one we use at Malai, and the only one I recommend.

HONEY • MAPLE SYRUP • LIGHT CORN SYRUP

To make a very creamy ice cream, you will need to use an invert sugar, or liquid sugar. This will make your ice cream smoother and more scoopable and reduce iciness. It's important! Although at Malai we use a specialized form of inverted sugar, more readily available liquid sweeteners like honey, grade A maple syrup, and light corn syrup can be used for the same purpose. I know that light corn syrup gets a bad rap, but the nice thing about it is that it imparts no flavor if flavor is not needed. These three liquid sweeteners can all replace one another in the recipes, so if you want to use maple syrup in all of your ice creams, go for it. If honey is your thing, that will work too. Just don't leave out this ingredient. It makes a world of difference in your end product.

FAVORITE TOOLS

These tools will be of immense help as you make the recipes in this book and will ensure that you have ice cream on hand whenever you want! Have a spice grinder and a mortar and pestle at your disposal to ensure the freshest ground spices, never be without a rubber spatula for stirring and folding all kinds of mixtures, and, most important of all, why not make ice cream with your ice cream maker every day?

MICROPLANE GRATER

I often say that if I were sent into exile on a deserted island, I would take my microplane grater with me, and that's no exaggeration. It is one of the most underrated items in the kitchen toolbox yet can do so much. It can grate moist fresh ginger or a hard spice like nutmeg or star anise, and it masterfully grates the zest of a lemon. It can even grate garlic, which is not relevant for this book, but I want to showcase its multitasking brilliance. You will find yourself picking up this versatile tool for dozens of tasks in this book and for your everyday cooking too.

SPOON

I wanted to say "offset spatula" here, but then I realized that I use a spoon whenever I need an offset and don't have one. You can use a spoon to frost cakes and glaze desserts. You can top off a pie with whipped cream with a spoon, and you can dump in some freshly grated spices with a spoon. You can open a jar with a spoon, and you can hold a wobbly table stable with a spoon. And more than anything else, you can taste with a spoon. A lot of people have flowers in the center of their dining table, but my family? We have a container of spoons. I know you have a spoon in your kitchen, but show it the love it deserves.

RUBBER SPATULA

You may not think much of this suggestion, but that's probably because you don't realize how much a good rubber spatula can change your life. We've all had the bad flimsy ones, and they do get the job done. But a good rubber spatula—one that is sturdy to the touch and holds firm—can ensure that you are leaving no ice cream behind as you scrape out every last bit and can also take on the tough job of mixing a dough (see Ice Cream Peda, page 152). Once you convert to a good rubber spatula, you'll never look back.

MORTAR AND PESTLE

If you haven't already guessed, I am a person who loves tradition. I even have a nostalgia for things that I never got to experience. So it will come as no surprise that I love a good mortar and pestle. After all, why do things the easy way when the traditional way is still available to you? (There are many reasons, but stick with me here.) I, of course, have the exact mortar and pestle that my mom has from India, but these two simple tools are available everywhere. They are great for crushing cardamom pods, black peppercorns, and fennel seeds, and I love the irregular bits and pieces that they produce. This is great for when you steep spices in an ice cream base and you just want to open them up to bring out their oils but don't need them finely ground.

COFFEE GRINDER

Why would you do things manually when an easier way is presented to you? I never ask myself this question. But I do have a spice grinder, and I do love it. Actually, scratch that. I don't have a spice grinder, but I do have a coffee grinder that I use only for spices. It's great for hard spices, such as cinnamon and star anise, because it grinds them to a fine powder for using in baked goods and in ice cream bases that don't need straining.

ICE CREAM MAKER

This seems obvious, but when making ice cream, it's nice to have an ice cream maker. Most electric ice cream makers fall into two main types, frozen bowl (aka canister) and compressor, but there are many different brands, which range widely in price and effectiveness. To produce the smoothest ice cream possible, try to find a unit that takes the least amount of time to churn the ice cream. This produces the smallest ice crystals, so when you freeze the ice cream, you are left with a luscious, smooth texture. The machines that typically take the shortest amount of time are usually the most expensive. But if you have a longer-running machine, no worries at all. The best time to eat your ice cream will be right after you churn it!

SPOUTED MEASURING CUP

A spouted measuring cup (aka liquid measuring cup) is a dream because it achieves two things at once: it measures and it pours. This may not amaze you as much as it does me, but measuring and pouring are two vital process steps in preparing ice cream, and a spouted measuring cup makes them easier. If you can, invest in a set in different sizes.

FREEZER-SAFE CONTAINERS

There are containers, and then there are freezer-safe containers. After making the recipes in this book, you'll likely sometimes have leftovers that you will need to store, and for that you'll need storage containers. You'll want to get something that snaps firmly shut so no air can enter and that won't shatter or crack if dropped. Only then will the ice cream taste like it did the day you made it.

ICE CREAM STORAGE & TRANSPORT

How you store ice cream is just as important as how you make it. Opening and closing your kitchen freezer causes a big temperature change and can affect whatever you are storing. In the case of ice cream, that temperature fluctuation creates not-so-pleasant ice crystals on top. To avoid that, store your ice cream in the back of your freezer. It's the coldest part and will be the least susceptible to the temperature changes. (But honestly, you should just eat your ice cream as fast as you can!)

The same rule applies to transporting ice cream. You want to make sure that it is not exposed to too many temperature changes. How you pack your ice cream for transport will depend on how long you will be in transit. If you will be traveling for 30 minutes or less, you can tote your ice cream in a regular shopping bag. For periods of 30 to 60 minutes, it's best to place the ice cream in an insulated bag. For 1 to 2 hours, put the ice cream in a cooler filled to the top with ice. This advice is good for pints or quarts of ice cream but will not work for ice cream desserts, such as ice cream cakes or pies.

For travel times of over 2 hours, purchase dry ice, put the ice cream in a cooler, and place the dry ice on top of the ice cream. Or better yet, make the ice cream once you get to your destination. Fresh ice cream always tastes the best!

Dairy Ice Cream
& Frozen Treats

Sweet Milk Ice Cream

The key to really great ice cream is a really great ice cream base, and this is the one for all of our dairy ice creams at Malai. Several things set it apart from the rest: it's incredibly milky, it has a full mouthfeel but is not too fatty, it finishes with a cooked caramel taste, and it's light and creamy—all at the same time. In my mind, it's perfect, and now it's yours.

MAKES 1½ QUARTS

1 tablespoon cornstarch

2 cups whole milk

3 tablespoons cream cheese, at room temperature

¼ teaspoon salt

1¼ cups heavy cream

¾ cup granulated cane sugar

2 tablespoons honey

❶ In a small bowl, mix the cornstarch with 2 tablespoons of the milk to make a slurry. Whisk the cream cheese and salt into the slurry until smooth. Set aside.

❷ In a saucepan, combine the remaining milk, the cream, sugar, and honey and bring to a boil over medium heat, whisking constantly to dissolve the sugar. Continue to boil, whisking constantly, until everything is well incorporated, about 3 minutes. Reduce the heat to low and whisk in the cornstarch slurry, mixing well. Raise the heat to medium, bring to a boil, and boil until slightly thickened, about 1 minute. Remove from the heat and transfer to a heatproof container.

❸ Let the base cool to room temperature, then cover tightly and refrigerate for at least 4 hours. (If you have the time, letting it sit in the refrigerator overnight is ideal.)

❹ Remove the chilled base from the refrigerator and stir to recombine. Transfer the base to your ice cream maker and churn according to the manufacturer's instructions. Serve the soft ice cream right away, or place in the freezer to freeze completely.

Rose with Cinnamon Roasted Almonds Ice Cream

This is the *most* popular Malai ice cream flavor. It's the only one we never take off the menu. When I created this flavor, which was very early on in the Malai journey, I was unsure about launching it. Rose ice cream was something that was ubiquitous in my childhood, so it makes me nostalgic. But were New Yorkers ready for something *this* new? I wasn't sure—until I absolutely was. This flavor's constant reign at the top never ceases to amaze me. And the best part? It's pink!

MAKES 1½ QUARTS

1 tablespoon cornstarch

1¼ cups heavy cream

3 tablespoons cream cheese, at room temperature

½ teaspoon ground cinnamon

¼ teaspoon table salt

2 cups whole milk

½ cup granulated cane sugar

¼ cup rose syrup (see Pooja's Tip)

2 tablespoons unsalted butter

¾ cup chopped almonds

¼ teaspoon fine sea salt

❶ In a small bowl, mix the cornstarch with 3 tablespoons of the cream to make a slurry. Whisk the cream cheese, cinnamon, and salt into the slurry until smooth. Set aside.

❷ In a saucepan, combine the remaining cream, the milk, sugar, and rose syrup and bring to a rolling boil over medium heat, whisking constantly to dissolve the sugar. Continue to boil, whisking constantly, until everything is well incorporated, about 4 minutes. Remove from the heat and whisk in the cornstarch slurry, mixing well.

❸ Return the mixture to a boil over medium heat and boil, stirring, until slightly thickened, about 1 minute. Remove from the heat and transfer to a heatproof container.

❹ Let the base cool to room temperature, then cover tightly and refrigerate for at least 4 hours to chill. (If you have the time, letting it sit in the refrigerator overnight is ideal.)

❺ While the mixture is cooling, prepare the almonds. In a small frying pan, melt the butter over medium heat. Add the almonds and stir until toasted and a shade darker, 3–4 minutes. Sprinkle with the sea salt, remove from the heat, and let cool completely.

❻ Remove the chilled base from the refrigerator and stir to recombine. Transfer the base to your ice cream maker and churn according to the manufacturer's instructions, adding the almonds during the last 5 minutes of churning. Serve the soft ice cream right away, or place in the freezer to freeze completely.

POOJA'S TIP

Rose syrup can be found at Indian grocery stores and online. Hamdard Rooh Afza, a widely distributed patented rose syrup, is the best-known brand, but other brands can be used. Do not substitute rose water or rose extract for the rose syrup.

POOJA'S TIP

You can use peeled or unpeeled ginger here. If you use unpeeled, be sure to scrub it very well!

Ginger Root Ice Cream

For years, I hosted a vegetarian Friendsgiving, and because my love of desserts was well known, I was always in charge of preparing them. One year, I decided to make, rather than buy, the ice creams to go along with the desserts, and one of them was a fresh ginger ice cream. The zingy spiciness and heady warmth of the ginger paired perfectly with the sweet, creamy ice cream base. My friends were blown away, and I had the idea that sparked Malai!

MAKES 1½ QUARTS

3½ ounces fresh ginger

1 tablespoon cornstarch

1¼ cups plus 3 tablespoons heavy cream

¼ teaspoon salt

2 cups whole milk

⅔ cup granulated cane sugar

2 tablespoons honey

1 Cut the ginger into long, 1-inch strips and transfer to a small saucepan. Add water just to cover the ginger and bring to a boil over medium-high heat. Boil for exactly 2 minutes, then remove from the heat and drain well. Set the ginger aside.

2 In a small bowl, mix the cornstarch with 3 tablespoons of the cream to make a slurry. Whisk the salt into the slurry and set aside.

3 In a saucepan, combine the remaining 1¼ cups cream, the milk, sugar, honey, and the reserved ginger and bring to a rolling boil over medium heat, whisking constantly to dissolve the sugar. Continue to boil, whisking constantly, until everything is well incorporated, about 4 minutes. Remove from the heat and whisk in the cornstarch slurry, mixing well.

4 Return the mixture to a boil over medium heat and boil, stirring, until slightly thickened, about 1 minute. Remove from the heat and let cool to room temperature.

5 Strain the base through a fine-mesh sieve into a container, cover tightly, and refrigerate for at least 6 hours. (If you have the time, letting it sit in the refrigerator overnight is ideal.)

6 Remove the chilled base from the refrigerator and stir to recombine. Transfer the base to your ice cream maker and churn according to the manufacturer's instructions. Serve the soft ice cream right away, or place in the freezer to freeze completely.

Star Anise Ice Cream

If you thought I made only Ginger Ice Cream for that Friendsgiving (see page 35), you're wrong. I made two flavors, and the second one was this equally delicious star anise–infused ice cream. I cannot say enough good things about the mellow licorice flavor this spice releases when mixed with dairy and sugar. It's subtle and perfect. At Malai, this flavor is on the menu as scoops and in our ice cream sando with Malai's Perfect Chocolate Chip Cookies (page 164), which carry their own hint of star anise.

MAKES 1½ QUARTS

1 tablespoon cornstarch

1¼ cups plus 3 tablespoons heavy cream

¼ teaspoon salt

2 cups whole milk

⅔ cup granulated cane sugar

2 tablespoons honey

4–5 whole star anise

❶ In a small bowl, mix the cornstarch with 3 tablespoons of the cream to make a slurry. Whisk in the salt and set aside.

❷ In a saucepan, combine the remaining 1¼ cups cream, the milk, sugar, honey, and star anise and bring to a rolling boil over medium heat, whisking constantly to dissolve the sugar. Continue to boil, whisking constantly, until everything is well incorporated, about 4 minutes. Remove from the heat and whisk in the cornstarch slurry, mixing well.

❸ Return the mixture to a boil over medium heat and boil, stirring, until slightly thickened, about 1 minute. Remove from the heat and let cool to room temperature.

❹ Strain the cooled base through a fine-mesh sieve into a container, cover tightly, and refrigerate for at least 6 hours. (If you have the time, letting it sit in the refrigerator overnight is ideal.)

❺ Remove the chilled base from the refrigerator and stir to recombine. Transfer the base to your ice cream maker and churn according to the manufacturer's instructions. Serve the soft ice cream right away, or place in the freezer to freeze completely.

Coffee Cardamom Ice Cream

Some pairings are meant to go together: peanut butter and bananas; saffron and pistachios; and of course coffee and cardamom. These two ingredients play off of each other especially well, with bitterness and acidity of the coffee and the bright floral qualities of cardamom heightening each other. One of the first flavors that I created for Malai, this ice cream quickly became one of our most popular and is now one of our most readily available pints. Top a scoop with chocolate sauce for a mocha note.

MAKES 1½ QUARTS

2 cups whole milk

1 tablespoon cornstarch

3 tablespoons cream cheese, at room temperature

¼ teaspoon salt

1¼ cups heavy cream

⅓ cup granulated cane sugar

⅓ cup packed dark brown sugar

2 tablespoons honey

1 tablespoon instant espresso powder

1 teaspoon ground cardamom

❶ In a small bowl, mix 2 tablespoons of the milk with the cornstarch to make a slurry. Whisk the cream cheese and salt into the slurry until smooth. Set aside.

❷ In a saucepan, combine the remaining milk, the cream, granulated and brown sugars, honey, espresso powder, and cardamom and bring to a boil over medium heat, whisking constantly to dissolve the sugars. Continue to boil, whisking constantly, until everything is well incorporated, about 3 minutes. Reduce the heat to low and whisk in the cornstarch slurry, mixing well. Raise the heat to medium, bring to a boil, and boil, stirring, until slightly thickened, about 1 minute. Remove from the heat and transfer to a heatproof container.

❸ Let the base cool to room temperature, then cover tightly and refrigerate for at least 4 hours. (If you have the time, letting it sit in the refrigerator overnight is ideal.)

❹ Remove the chilled base from the refrigerator and stir to recombine. Transfer the base to your ice cream maker and churn according to the manufacturer's instructions. Serve the soft ice cream right away, or place in the freezer to freeze completely.

Masala Chai Ice Cream

Masala chai, or spiced tea, is perhaps the single most influential drink in my life. My parents, for whom chai is a daily (if not twice a day) ritual, started giving me and my sister sips of this sweet, spiced drink, diluted with milk, at a very early age. And it was this balance—the dairy with the spices, the bitterness of the tea, and the sweetness of sugar—that was my entry into the world of flavor integration, Indian cuisine, and spices. What I know is that my life would have been very different if not for masala chai. And your life will change with this Masala Chai Ice Cream.

MAKES 1½ QUARTS

---

2 ounces fresh ginger

1 tablespoon cornstarch

1¼ cups plus 3 tablespoons heavy cream

¼ teaspoon salt

2 cups whole milk

⅔ cup granulated cane sugar

2 tablespoons honey

2 tablespoons chai masala (see Malai Fun Fact)

¼ cup loose CTC black tea (see Pooja's Tip)

MALAI FUN FACT

My family's blend of chai spices (which is what we use at Malai) is ginger and black pepper heavy, with notes of cinnamon, cardamom, and clove. That said, the spice proportion can be adjusted based on preference. If you do not have a jar of Malai Chai Masala on hand, feel free to use any tea spices you do have. Pumpkin pie spice will also work in a pinch.

❶ Cut the ginger into long, 1-inch strips and transfer to a small saucepan. Add water just to cover the ginger and bring to a boil over medium-high heat. Boil for exactly 2 minutes, then remove from the heat and drain well. Set the ginger aside.

❷ In a small bowl, mix the cornstarch with 3 tablespoons of the cream to make a slurry. Whisk in the salt and set aside.

❸ In a saucepan, combine the remaining 1¼ cups cream, the milk, sugar, honey, ginger, and chai masala and bring to a rolling boil over medium heat, whisking to dissolve the sugar. Continue to boil, whisking constantly, until everything is well incorporated, about 4 minutes. Remove from the heat and whisk in the cornstarch slurry, mixing well.

❹ Return the mixture to a boil over medium heat, add the CTC tea, and boil, stirring, until slightly thickened and the mixture has turned a deep amber, about 1 minute. Remove from the heat, strain into a heat-proof bowl, and let cool to room temperature.

❺ Cover tightly, and refrigerate for at least 4 hours. (If you have the time, letting it sit in the refrigerator overnight is ideal.)

❻ Remove the chilled base from the refrigerator and stir to recombine. Transfer the base to your ice cream maker and churn according to the manufacturer's instructions. Serve the soft ice cream right away, or place in the freezer to freeze completely.

POOJA'S TIP

CTC black tea—which stands for crush, tear, curl (a method of processing tea)—is traditionally used for making masala chai. It's a homogenized black tea that produces a beautiful red-amber color when brewed. Your favorite black tea can be used in place of the CTC tea.

Jaggery Ice Cream

A stereotype recognized among Indian subcultures is that Gujaratis (my family's subculture) tend to like their food sweet. Indeed, we Gujaratis add sweetness to our lentils and other savory dishes, and if there isn't any sweetness in the main meal, we have a piece of jaggery, an unrefined cane sugar with a rich caramel flavor (see page 18), on our plate to eat with everything else. I am very pleased to say that I fit quite nicely into this sweet-loving subculture. Jaggery is also amazing in ice cream, which you will discover when you churn this recipe.

MAKES 1 QUART

1 tablespoon cornstarch

2 cups whole milk

3 tablespoons cream cheese, at room temperature

½ teaspoon salt

1¼ cups heavy cream

¾ cup powdered jaggery (or ⅔ cup if shaved from the block; see Pooja's Tip)

2 tablespoons honey

1 In a small bowl, mix the cornstarch with 2 tablespoons of the milk to make a slurry. Whisk the cream cheese and salt into the slurry until smooth. Set aside.

2 In a saucepan, combine the remaining milk, the cream, jaggery, and honey and bring to a boil over medium heat, whisking constantly to dissolve the jaggery. Continue to boil, whisking constantly, until the jaggery has fully melted and everything is well incorporated, about 3 minutes. Reduce the heat to low and whisk in the cornstarch slurry, mixing well. Raise the heat to medium, bring to a boil, and boil, whisking constantly, until slightly thickened, about 1 minute. Remove from the heat and transfer to a heatproof container.

3 Let the base cool to room temperature, then cover tightly and refrigerate for at least 4 hours. (If you have the time, letting it sit in the refrigerator overnight is ideal.)

4 Remove the chilled base from the refrigerator and stir to recombine. Transfer the base to your ice cream maker and churn according to the manufacturer's instructions. Serve the soft ice cream right away, or place in the freezer to freeze completely.

POOJA'S TIP

Jaggery is readily available in Indian grocery stores and online. You'll see powdered versions (similar to brown sugar) and block versions, which must be shaved into a powder with a knife. Either works in this recipe.

Mango & Cream Ice Cream

A summertime staple for my family is dudh keri, a dessert that my mom makes. She chops up ripe, peak-season mangoes, covers them with sweetened milk, and chills the whole thing. That time in the refrigerator is where the magic happens. The mangoes and the milk marry, and the mangoes become sweeter while the milk becomes ever so slightly mango flavored. The result is incredible. In ice cream form, I alternated layers of my Sweet Milk Ice Cream (page 31), still soft from the maker, with mango purée, which seeps into the ice cream layers to create a lightly flavored mango ice cream.

MAKES 1½ QUARTS

---

2 cups whole milk

1 tablespoon cornstarch

3 tablespoons cream cheese, at room temperature

¼ teaspoon salt

1¼ cups heavy cream

¾ cup granulated cane sugar

2 tablespoons honey

1 cup mango purée (see Pooja's Tip)

❶ In a small bowl, mix 2 tablespoons of the milk with the cornstarch to make a slurry. Whisk the cream cheese and salt into the slurry until smooth. Set aside.

❷ In a saucepan, combine the remaining milk, the cream, sugar, and honey and bring to a boil over medium heat, whisking constantly to dissolve the sugar. Continue to boil, whisking constantly, until everything is well incorporated, about 3 minutes. Reduce the heat to low and whisk in the cornstarch slurry, mixing well. Raise the heat to medium, bring to a boil, and boil, stirring, until slightly thickened, about 1 minute. Remove from the heat and transfer to a heatproof container.

❸ Let the base cool to room temperature, then cover tightly and refrigerate for at least 4 hours. (If you have the time, letting it sit in the refrigerator overnight is ideal.)

❹ Remove the chilled base from the refrigerator and stir to recombine. Transfer the base to your ice cream maker and churn according to the manufacturer's instructions. Remove about one-fourth of the ice cream from the machine and layer it on the bottom of a freezer-safe container. Add about ¼ cup of the mango purée, then continue alternating layers of ice cream and purée until you've used both of them up, finishing with a layer of ice cream. Serve the soft ice cream right away, or place in the freezer to freeze completely.

POOJA'S TIP

When shopping for mango purée, look for a product with no added sugar.

Orange Fennel Ice Cream

Look, I don't play favorites with my Malai ice cream babies. They're all wonderful, and I love each one equally. But if I could eat only one for a year, this just might be my choice. It's refreshing, it's unexpected, and it's zesty and warm. It was also one of the first ice cream flavors I created, so it has a special place in my heart. Just don't tell the other flavors, okay?

MAKES 1½ QUARTS

2 cups whole milk

1 tablespoon cornstarch

¼ teaspoon salt

1¼ cups heavy cream

⅔ cup granulated cane sugar

2 tablespoons light corn syrup

1½ tablespoons fennel seeds

Grated zest of 1 orange

❶ In a small bowl, mix 2 tablespoons of the milk with the cornstarch and salt to make a slurry. Set aside.

❷ In a saucepan, combine the remaining milk, the cream, sugar, corn syrup, fennel seeds, and orange zest and bring to a boil over medium heat, whisking constantly to dissolve the sugar. Continue to boil, whisking constantly, until everything is well incorporated, about 3 minutes. Reduce the heat to low and whisk in the cornstarch slurry, mixing well. Raise the heat to medium, bring to a boil, and boil, stirring, until slightly thickened, about 1 minute. Remove from the heat and let cool to room temperature.

❸ Strain the cooled based through a fine-mesh sieve into a container, cover tightly, and refrigerate for at least 4 hours. (If you have the time, letting it sit in the refrigerator overnight is ideal.)

❹ Remove the chilled based from the refrigerator and stir to recombine. Transfer the base to your ice cream maker and churn according to the manufacturer's instructions. Serve the soft ice cream right away, or place in the freezer to freeze completely.

Golden Turmeric Ice Cream

For me, turmeric has always signified a cure to an ailment. Have a cold? Mix turmeric with hot water and lemon juice and drink it up. Trouble sleeping? Mix turmeric with warm milk and honey and head to bed. Feeling fatigued and unwell overall? Just consume a daily spoonful of turmeric. So when turmeric started becoming more prevalent in Western desserts, I was intrigued. Something I used to make myself feel better . . . in a dessert? But then I tried it in ice cream and realized how delicious it could be! I still turn to turmeric when I'm feeling a bit off, but I'd rather just have a scoop of this ice cream.

MAKES 1½ QUARTS

2 ounces fresh ginger

1 tablespoon cornstarch

1¼ cups plus 3 tablespoons heavy cream

3 tablespoons cream cheese, at room temperature

¼ teaspoon salt

2 cups whole milk

1 cup granulated cane sugar

2 tablespoons honey

2 teaspoons ground turmeric

½ teaspoon ground cinnamon

½ teaspoon ground black pepper

❶ Cut the ginger into long, 1-inch strips and transfer to a small saucepan. Add water just to cover the ginger and bring to a boil over medium-high heat. Boil for exactly 2 minutes, then remove from heat and drain well. Set the ginger aside.

❷ In a small bowl, mix the cornstarch with 3 tablespoons of the cream to make a slurry. Whisk the cream cheese and salt into the slurry until smooth. Set aside.

❸ In a saucepan, combine the remaining 1¼ cups cream, the milk, sugar, honey, turmeric, cinnamon, pepper, and reserved ginger and whisk to mix. Bring to a rolling boil over medium heat, whisking constantly to dissolve the sugar. Continue to boil, whisking constantly, until everything is well incorporated, about 4 minutes. Remove from the heat and whisk in the cornstarch slurry, mixing well.

❹ Return the mixture to a boil over medium heat and boil, stirring, until slightly thickened, about 1 minute. Remove from the heat and let cool to room temperature.

❺ Strain the cooled base through a fine-mesh sieve into a container, cover tightly, and refrigerate for at least 4 hours. (If you have the time, letting it sit in the refrigerator overnight is ideal.)

❻ Remove the chilled base from the refrigerator and stir to recombine. Transfer the base to your ice cream maker and churn according to the manufacturer's instructions. Serve the soft ice cream right away, or place in the freezer to freeze completely.

Salted Browned Butter Pecan Ice Cream

Growing up, I always underappreciated butter pecan ice cream, and I think it was for good reason. There was a promise of pecans and, well, butter, but those store-bought containers in the 1990s never really had either. It was most often vanilla ice cream with what seemed like a nut or two. When I realized the true potential of butter pecan ice cream, I set out to make a great version. I used browned butter to play up the nutty flavor and threw in lots and lots of toasted pecans. Here's the result of my efforts, which is the very best version of this popular ice cream I've ever tasted.

MAKES 1 QUART

⅓ cup granulated cane sugar

⅓ cup packed dark brown sugar

1 tablespoon pure vanilla extract or vanilla bean paste

1 teaspoon salt

1 cup whole milk

2 cups heavy cream

4 tablespoons unsalted butter

1 cup pecans, finely chopped

❶ In a bowl, whisk together the granulated and brown sugars, vanilla, ¼ teaspoon of the salt, and the milk until the sugars have dissolved. Stir in the cream. Cover tightly and refrigerate for at least 2 hours. (If you have the time, letting it sit in the refrigerator overnight is ideal.)

❷ At least 1 hour before churning the ice cream, in a small pan, melt the butter over medium-low heat. Once it has melted, it will foam and then the foam will subside and little brown bits will start forming on the bottom of the pan. Immediately add the pecans and the remaining ¾ teaspoon salt and stir well, scraping along the bottom of the pan. Cook, stirring frequently, until the pecans are toasted, about 8 minutes. Remove from the heat and let cool completely.

❸ Remove the chilled base from the refrigerator and stir to recombine. Transfer the base to your ice cream maker and churn according to the manufacturer's instructions, adding the pecans during the last 5 minutes of churning. Serve the soft ice cream right away, or place in the freezer to freeze completely.

MALAI FUN FACT

This flavor was part of Malai's lineup for the first few years and is now safely in the Malai archives. We make it in-house from time to time for a quick team indulgence.

Fenugreek Ice Cream with Walnuts

I love when I can reference my hybrid identity in a spice. Stick with me, here. Take fenugreek—in Indian cooking, it adds a subtle bitter nuance to savory dishes. But it also has a sweetness that unmistakably tastes like maple syrup! Seeing this spice in a whole new light, as nutty and toasty and sweet, is what I like to call an amazing spice discovery.

MAKES 1½ QUARTS

FOR THE ICE CREAM BASE

1 tablespoon cornstarch

2 cups whole milk

3 tablespoons cream cheese, at room temperature

¼ teaspoon salt

1¼ cups heavy cream

⅔ cup granulated cane sugar

2 tablespoons grade A maple syrup

1½ tablespoons ground fenugreek (see Pooja's Tip)

FOR THE NUT INCLUSION

¾ cup chopped walnuts

2 tablespoons unsalted butter

½ teaspoon salt

❶ To make the ice cream base, in a small bowl, mix the cornstarch with 2 tablespoons of the milk to make a slurry. Whisk the cream cheese and salt into the slurry until smooth. Set aside.

❷ In a saucepan, combine the remaining milk, the cream, sugar, maple syrup, and fenugreek powder and bring to a boil over medium heat, whisking constantly to dissolve the sugar. Continue to boil, whisking constantly, until everything is well incorporated, about 3 minutes. Reduce the heat to low and whisk in the cornstarch slurry, mixing well. Raise the heat to medium, bring to a boil, and boil, stirring, until slightly thickened, about 1 minute. Remove from the heat and transfer to a heatproof container.

❸ Let the base cool to room temperature, then cover tightly and refrigerate for at least 4 hours. (If you have the time, letting it sit in the refrigerator overnight is ideal.)

4 Meanwhile, prepare the nut inclusion. In a nonstick frying pan, stir together the walnuts, butter, and salt, making sure all the nuts are coated with butter. Place over medium-high heat and toast, stirring often, until the mixture smells nutty, 5–7 minutes. Remove from the heat and let cool completely. Transfer to an airtight container and keep at room temperature until ready to use.

5 Remove the chilled base from the refrigerator and stir to recombine. Transfer the base to your ice cream maker and churn according to the manufacturer's instructions. Once the mixture has frozen to a soft consistency, using a rubber spatula, fold in the walnuts, distributing them evenly.

6 Serve the soft ice cream right away, or and place in the freezer to freeze completely.

POOJA'S TIP

To make ground fenugreek, in a spice grinder or coffee grinder, grind ¼ cup fenugreek seeds to a fine powder. Store any ground fenugreek not needed for this recipe in an airtight jar in a cool cupboard. Fenugreek seeds can be found in specialty food stores, Indian grocery stores, or online.

White Chocolate Cheesecake Ice Cream

My first baking adventure happened when I was ten years old. I was watching one of the first iterations of food television and saw a show where Mrs. Fields—of national cookie-chain fame—was making a white chocolate cheesecake. I love white chocolate (controversial, I know), so everything about this cheesecake was calling my name. I made it and it was a disaster, yet everyone in my family loved it anyway. I have a distinct memory of thinking about how when I made something with my hard work and was intended to be enjoyed, it was loved. I started Malai years later, but this memory has always remained as one that helped to start me on this journey.

MAKES 1 QUART

FOR THE CRUST INCLUSION

½ cup graham cracker crumbs (from 7 squares) (see Pooja's Tip, page 144)

¼ cup granulated cane sugar

½ teaspoon salt

4 tablespoons unsalted butter, melted

FOR THE ICE CREAM BASE

1 package (8 ounces) cream cheese, at room temperature

⅔ cup granulated cane sugar

2 cups heavy cream

1 cup whole milk

½ cup white chocolate chips, melted and cooled, plus ½ cup whole white chocolate chips

❶ To make the crust inclusion, in a bowl, mix together the graham cracker crumbs, sugar, salt, and butter until the mixture is evenly moistened and forms clumps. Set aside.

❷ To make the ice cream base, in a blender, combine the cream cheese, sugar, cream, milk, and melted white chocolate and blend on high speed until the mixture is smooth, about 1½ minutes.

❸ Transfer the base to your ice cream maker and churn according to the manufacturer's instructions. Once the mixture has frozen to a soft-serve consistency, evenly sprinkle in the whole white chocolate chips and the graham cracker crumb mixture. Using a rubber spatula, fold in both inclusions, distributing them evenly.

❹ Serve the soft ice cream right away, or place in the freezer to freeze completely.

POOJA'S TIP

Ground cumin is readily available in supermarkets. But to amp up this flavor, I recommend buying Burlap & Barrel Wild Mountain cumin seeds, which are smoky, aromatic, and so flavorful. Grind those whole seeds in a spice grinder for the freshest possible cumin flavor.

Raspberry Cumin Ice Cream

Here is the truth about this flavor. We introduced it to the Malai lineup a few years ago. Our customers were intrigued, tasted it, and loved the woodsy notes of cumin with the tart sweetness of raspberries! It was midsummer—our busiest season—so we tweaked the recipe a bit, wrote it down, and moved on with the rest of our summer. To this day, we cannot find that sheet of paper. Fortunately, after a lot of testing, I was able to recreate it for you here. Our beloved raspberry-cumin combo is back.

MAKES 1½ QUARTS

FOR THE CUMIN ICE CREAM

1 tablespoon cornstarch

1¼ cups plus 3 tablespoons heavy cream

¼ teaspoon salt

2 cups whole milk

⅔ cup granulated cane sugar

2 tablespoons honey

1 tablespoon ground cumin (see Pooja's Tip)

FOR THE RASPBERRY SAUCE

1 pint (2 cups) fresh raspberries, or 1 bag (8 ounces) frozen raspberries

½ cup granulated cane sugar

1 tablespoon fresh lemon juice

Pinch of salt

1 To make the ice cream, in a small bowl, mix the cornstarch with 3 tablespoons of the cream to make a slurry. Whisk in the salt and set aside.

2 In a saucepan, combine the remaining 1¼ cups cream, the milk, sugar, honey, and cumin and bring to a rolling boil over medium heat, whisking constantly to dissolve the sugar. Continue to boil, whisking constantly, until everything is well incorporated, about 4 minutes. Remove from the heat and whisk in the cornstarch slurry, mixing well.

3 Return the mixture to a boil over medium heat and boil, stirring, until slightly thickened, about 1 minute. Remove from the heat and transfer to a heatproof container.

4 Let the base cool to room temperature, then cover tightly and refrigerate for 12 hours.

5 Meanwhile, make the raspberry sauce. In a blender, combine the raspberries, sugar, lemon juice, and salt and blend until smooth. If seeds or other bits are visible, strain the sauce through a fine-mesh sieve. You should have about ⅔ cup. Refrigerate in a tightly covered container until ready to use.

6 Remove the chilled base from the refrigerator and stir to recombine. Transfer the base to your ice cream maker and churn according to the manufacturer's instructions. Remove about one-fourth of the ice cream from the machine and layer it on the bottom of a freezer-safe container. Add about ¼ cup of the raspberry sauce, then continue alternating layers of ice cream and sauce until you've used both of them up, finishing with a layer of ice cream. Serve the soft ice cream right away, or place in the freezer to freeze completely.

Apricot Mace Sherbet

For an embarrassingly long time, I did not know that apricots were actually fruit—I mean, a piece of fruit you can eat. I thought apricot was just a flavor. Apricot baby food (a favorite even after I was old enough not to eat baby food), apricot jam, dried apricots (that's right, I didn't realize they were the actual fruit)—I never thought that all of these things came from something fresh. I'm clearly a product of the processed-food revolution. I now know that the fresh fruit exists, but to ensure that the season lasts just a bit longer, I use store-bought apricot purée instead of the fruit for this sherbet. The taste of pure apricot enhanced with the sweet, bright notes of mace—this flavor is very real.

MAKES 1½ QUARTS

½ cup whole milk

½ cup heavy cream

2½ cups apricot purée

1½ cups granulated cane sugar

¼ cup light corn syrup

1 teaspoon ground mace (see Pooja's Tip)

1 In a large bowl, using an electric mixer, beat together the milk, cream, apricot purée, sugar, corn syrup, and mace on medium speed until well blended, about 2 minutes.

2 Transfer the mixture to your ice cream maker and churn according to the manufacturer's instructions. Serve the soft sherbet right away, or place in the freezer to freeze completely.

POOJA'S TIP

The outer lacy coating (blade) of the nutmeg seed, mace has the same bright, warm, nutty flavors as nutmeg but with unmistakable fruity notes that are perfect for this sherbet. Ground mace is available in most grocery stores, or you can buy mace blades and grind them in your spice grinder for a fresher flavor.

Watermelon Sherbet

One of my favorite summertime frozen treats growing up was a Friendly's *Wattamelon Roll*. It had a thin outer layer of green lime sherbet, followed by a layer of white lemon sherbet, and then the star of the show, a beautiful red watermelon sherbet studded with chocolate chips to mimic watermelon seeds—all in the shape of a watermelon slice. My mouth is watering just thinking about that dessert. I don't have the patience to recreate it, but whipping up a watermelon sherbet is easy and makes the perfect warm-weather treat. Chocolate chips are not optional!

MAKES 2 QUARTS

---

6 cups seedless watermelon cubes (from about ½ mini seedless watermelon)

1 can (14 ounces) sweetened condensed milk

2 tablespoons honey

½ teaspoon salt

¼ cup fresh lime juice

¾ cup mini chocolate chips, any kind

❶ In a blender, combine the watermelon, condensed milk, honey, salt, and lime juice and blend until completely smooth, about 2 minutes.

❷ Transfer the mixture to your ice cream maker and churn according to the manufacturer's instructions, adding the chocolate chips during the last 4 minutes of churning. Serve the soft sherbet right away, or place in the freezer to freeze completely.

Guava Ice Cream with Kashmiri Chili Powder

Even though guava-flavored ice cream has long been popular in India, I never gravitated toward it during my summer trips. I always went for my tried-and-true classic Indian favorites that I was unable to find at home: tender coconut, custard apple, and sapota. That remained true until I traveled to India not long ago and intentionally went out for ice cream every single day—this ice cream lover wanted to get all the ice creams in! Given my regimen, I eventually tried the guava. That was when I discovered what I had been missing out on for so many years. Tart and creamy with just a hint of spice, guava ice cream hooked me immediately, and I knew that I had to recreate it at home.

MAKES 1½ QUARTS

2 cups heavy cream

1 can (14 ounces) sweetened condensed milk

1½ cups pink guava purée

1 teaspoon Kashmiri red chili powder (see Pooja's Tip)

½ teaspoon salt

1 In a large bowl, using an electric mixer, beat the cream on medium-high speed until stiff peaks form, about 5 minutes. Using a rubber spatula, carefully fold in the condensed milk, guava purée, chili powder, and salt, incorporating them evenly.

2 Transfer the mixture to a freezer-safe storage container and freeze for at least 4 hours or up to overnight before serving.

POOJA'S TIP

Kashmiri red chili powder has a mild flavor but packs a punch with its dark red color. It can be found online and in Indian grocery stores. In a pinch, you can substitute cayenne pepper but reduce the amount to ½ teaspoon.

Raita Frozen Yogurt Sherbet

There is a reason why raita is present at so many Indian meals: it's the cooling antidote to the many spicy dishes that are typically consumed. So why not take that cooling component and—dare I say it—make it even cooler! This hybrid frozen yogurt and sherbet is likely not something you've ever tried. It is more savory than the usual sweet treats that are in this book, but that makes it all the more surprising, refreshing, and delicious—and it will absolutely cool you down.

MAKES 1 QUART

1 cup honey

1 cup plain whole-milk yogurt

½ cup heavy cream

¼ cup vodka

1 teaspoon ground cumin

2 English cucumbers, peeled and grated

1. In a large bowl, whisk together the honey, yogurt, cream, vodka, and cumin, mixing well. Using a rubber spatula, fold in the cucumber until evenly incorporated.

2. Transfer the mixture to your ice cream maker and churn according to the manufacturer's instructions. Serve the soft sherbet right away, or place in the freezer to freeze completely.

POOJA'S TIP

You may have noticed that this ice cream is a bit boozy! Alcohol has a low freezing temperature, so it's often used to reduce the amount of large ice crystals. Because this dessert does not have a lot of fat but does have quite a bit of water from the cucumbers, I needed to add something to offset the iciness. You can't taste it, but if you do not wish to add the vodka, no big deal! I'd just advise that you eat it right after it's churned.

Cardamom Kulfi Ice Pops

I will admit: this sweet treat is lifted directly from my mom's recipe book. She was not much of a dessert maker when we were growing up, but she had a few recipes in her sweets arsenal—both Indian and western—that were simply spectacular: gulab jamun, shrikhand, cheesecake, Granola Chocolate Chip Cookies (page 176), and kulfi. My mom makes the best kulfi on the planet—there is no question about that—and I wanted to share that kulfi love.

MAKES 8–10 ICE POPS

¾ teaspoon ground cardamom

1 tablespoon hot water

1½ cups heavy cream

1 can (12 ounces) evaporated milk

1 can (14 ounces) sweetened condensed milk

1. In a small bowl, mix together the cardamom and hot water.

2. In a large bowl, whisk together the cream, evaporated milk, condensed milk, and bloomed cardamom and whisk until well mixed.

3. Divide the mixture evenly among 8–10 ice-pop molds and freeze for at least 5 hours or up to overnight before serving.

Mishti Doi Frozen Yogurt

I hadn't heard of mishti doi, a jaggery-sweetened yogurt dish topped with a thin layer of ghee, until I was an adult during my first trip to the Eastern part of India. But when I discovered it, I was hooked: creamy, earthy, so wildly dairy-filled. It's easy to translate this into a frozen version, and here it is!

MAKES 1 QUART

1 cup powdered jaggery (see Pooja's Tip)

1½ cups plain whole-milk Greek yogurt

2 tablespoons ghee

½ teaspoon ground cardamom

¼ teaspoon salt

1 In a blender, combine the jaggery, yogurt, ghee, cardamom, and salt and blend until well mixed and smooth, 2–3 minutes.

2 Transfer the mixture to your ice cream maker and churn according to the manufacturer's instructions. Serve the soft frozen yogurt right away, or place in the freezer to freeze completely.

POOJA'S TIP

You'll want to use powdered jaggery for this recipe, rather than jaggery shaved from a block, as the powdered form will blend more easily into the yogurt.

Pistachio Soan Papdi Kulfi Ice Pops

Soan papdi is a confection that is meant to have you hooked. It's sweet and flaky, almost nougat-like, and it melts in your mouth. It's not easy to make it at home, but when you buy a box and incorporate it into delicious frozen desserts—like this pistachio kulfi—you're left with pockets of creamy, sugary, nutty bites of joy.

MAKES 8–10 ICE POPS

1½ cups heavy cream

1 can (12 ounces) evaporated milk

1 can (14 ounces) sweetened condensed milk

¼ cup pistachio butter (see Pooja's Tip)

¼ teaspoon salt

½ pound store-bought soan papdi

❶ In a blender, combine the cream, evaporated milk, condensed milk, pistachio butter, salt, and ¼ pound of the soan papdi and blend until smooth but not completely puréed, about 45 seconds.

❷ Divide the remaining ¼ pound soan papdi evenly among 8–10 ice-pop molds, then add the cream mixture to the molds, dividing it evenly. Freeze for at least 5 hours or up to overnight before serving.

POOJA'S TIP

Both pistachio butter and soan papdi can be found online. You can also find pistachio butter at specialty food stores and soan papdi at Indian grocery stores.

Mango Lassi Ice Pops

When our family goes out to eat at an Indian restaurant, I never order mango lassi, but my dad always does. And inevitably, I will ask him for a sip, slowly moving the glass closer and closer to me until he eventually orders another one for himself and lets me have his original one. This happens like clockwork. I never think mango lassi will be exciting, but then I have one sip and I remember that tangy yogurt with bright, sweet mango will literally never be bad. So always order that mango lassi when you're at an Indian restaurant, and make it in frozen form here using this recipe.

MAKES 8–10 ICE POPS

2 cups sweetened mango pulp (see Pooja's Tip)

1 cup plain whole-milk Greek yogurt

1 cup heavy cream

1 teaspoon ground cardamom

¼ teaspoon salt

❶ In a blender, combine the mango pulp, yogurt, cream, cardamom, and salt and blend until smooth, about 1½ minutes.

❷ Divide the mixture evenly among 8–10 ice-pop molds and freeze for at least 5 hours or up to overnight before serving.

POOJA'S TIP

Sweetened mango pulp, or aam ras, is imperative for this recipe. You cannot substitute any other kind of mango purée because the sweetness and the deep flavor of aam ras are necessary for these ice pops to taste great. You can find it online and at Indian grocery stores.

Shrikhand Frozen Yogurt

My aunt Mayamasi, my mom's younger sister, was one of my favorite people. She was my hype woman in every way, always believing that I could do anything. After she was diagnosed with ALS, she would tell me that she missed eating her favorite dessert, shrikhand, a thick, sweetened yogurt dish seasoned with saffron and studded with almonds. There is nothing not to love about this dessert, but I had never come across anyone who loved it more than Mayamasi, so I created this recipe in honor of her. She passed away before the launch of this flavor at Malai, but I know she would have loved it and hyped it in the way that only she could do.

MAKES 1 QUART

¼ **teaspoon packed saffron threads**

1 **tablespoon boiling water**

1 **quart plain whole-milk yogurt**

1 **cup granulated cane sugar**

1 **tablespoon honey**

½ **teaspoon salt**

½ **cup sliced almonds, toasted**

❶ To bloom the saffron, crush the saffron threads with your fingers and drop them into a small heatproof bowl. Add the boiling water and let sit to develop the flavor, at least 5 minutes or up to 20 minutes.

❷ In a bowl, whisk together the yogurt, sugar, honey, and salt, mixing well. Whisk in the bloomed saffron, blending evenly.

❸ Transfer the mixture to your ice cream maker and churn according to the manufacturer's instructions, adding the almonds during the last 3 minutes of churning. Serve the soft frozen yogurt right away, or place in the freezer to freeze completely.

Horlicks (Malted Milk) Ice Cream

Does everyone have a warm malted milk story? Because honestly, everyone should. Mine is this: I interned at a women's labor union in India the summer between my sophomore and junior years of college. And it happened to be in my parents' hometown, so I lived with my grandparents. My grandmother, Ba—she makes a few appearances in this book—was starting to slow down at the time. She didn't cook much anymore and rarely left the house, but every day, without fail, when I came home from my internship, I would find her in the kitchen making me a big (it was very big) mug of warm Horlicks, or malted milk. I would take it from her, we would walk out to the swing on the front porch, and I would tell her about my day and sip my milk. I never really *wanted* that milk, as it was a very heavy snack between lunch and dinner. But she loved making it for me, and I loved making her happy and cherished our daily alone time. Every time I see Horlicks now, I think of Ba and the steaming milk that was always waiting for me.

MAKES 1½ QUARTS

1 tablespoon cornstarch

1¼ cups plus 3 tablespoons heavy cream

¼ teaspoon fine sea salt

2 cups whole milk

¼ cup granulated cane sugar

¼ cup malted milk powder (preferably Horlicks)

2 tablespoons honey

❶ In a small bowl, mix the cornstarch with 3 tablespoons of the cream to make a slurry. Whisk in the salt and set aside.

❷ In a saucepan, combine the remaining 1¼ cups cream, the milk, sugar, malted milk powder, and honey and bring to a rolling boil over medium heat, whisking constantly to dissolve the sugar. Continue to boil, whisking constantly, until everything is well incorporated, about 4 minutes. Remove from the heat and whisk in the cornstarch slurry, mixing well.

❸ Return the mixture to a boil over medium heat and boil, stirring, until slightly thickened, about 1 minute. Remove from the heat and transfer to a heatproof container.

❹ Let the base cool to room temperature, then cover tightly and refrigerate for at least 4 hours. (If you have the time, letting it sit in the refrigerator overnight is ideal.)

❺ Remove the chilled base from the refrigerator and stir to recombine. Transfer the base to your ice cream maker and churn according to the manufacturer's instructions. Serve the soft ice cream right away, or place in the freezer to freeze completely.

Carrot Halwa Ice Cream

Plain and simple, this ice cream came to be at Malai because my dad only likes to eat his carrot halwa, a carrot pudding spiced with cardamom, with a scoop of vanilla ice cream on top. He's a bit extra like that (I know where I get it from). As he was enjoying this dish one day, I thought about how easily this dessert, already made by cooking carrots in milk, could be transformed into an ice cream. It tastes just like the dessert in frozen form. Needless to say, my dad is pleased.

MAKES 1½ QUARTS

1 cup loosely packed shredded carrots (from 1–1½ pounds carrots)

1 tablespoon ghee

1 teaspoon ground cardamom

1 tablespoon cornstarch

1¼ cups plus 3 tablespoons heavy cream

¼ teaspoon salt

2 cups whole milk

⅔ cup granulated cane sugar

2 tablespoons honey

1. In a saucepan over medium-high heat, combine the carrots, ghee, and cardamom and cook, stirring constantly, until the carrots are fully cooked through and a shade lighter in color, 6–7 minutes. Remove from the heat and set aside.

2. In a small bowl, mix the cornstarch with 3 tablespoons of the cream to make a slurry. Whisk in the salt and set aside.

3. In a saucepan, combine the remaining 1¼ cups cream, the milk, sugar, and honey and bring to a rolling boil over medium heat, whisking constantly to dissolve the sugar. Continue to boil, whisking constantly, until everything is well incorporated, about 4 minutes. Remove from the heat, whisk in the cornstarch slurry, and then stir in the carrot mixture.

4. Return the mixture to a boil over medium heat and boil, whisking constantly, until slightly thickened, about 1 minute. Remove from the heat and transfer to a heatproof container.

5. Let the base cool to room temperature, then cover tightly and refrigerate for at least 4 hours. (If you have the time, letting it sit in the refrigerator overnight is ideal.)

6. Remove the chilled base from the refrigerator and stir to recombine. Transfer the base to your ice cream maker and churn according to the manufacturer's instructions. Serve the ice cream right away, or place in the freezer to freeze completely.

MALAI FUN FACT

This remains one of the most popular flavors at Malai, especially during Diwali time.

Gulab Jamun Ice Cream

Our gulab jamun ice cream cakes have become a defining product for Malai: saffron syrup–soaked cardamom cakes sandwiching our Rose with Cinnamon Roasted Almonds Ice Cream (page 32). I wanted to provide the same qualities in an easier, non-cake-building version for this book. Enter, Gulab Jamun Ice Cream. Here, we are blending the syrupy doughnuts (store-bought!) directly into the spiced ice cream base, so you still get that milk-powdery, fried-flavor goodness and spiciness the dessert is known for.

MAKES 1½ QUARTS

¼ teaspoon packed saffron threads

1 tablespoon boiling water

1 tablespoon cornstarch

2 cups heavy cream

1¾ cups whole milk

⅔ cup granulated cane sugar

¼ cup light corn syrup

½ teaspoon ground cardamom

½ teaspoon salt

10 store-bought gulab jamun balls (see Pooja's Tip)

1 teaspoon rose water

1 To bloom the saffron, crush the saffron threads with your fingers and drop them into a small heatproof bowl. Add the boiling water and let sit to develop the flavor, at least 5 minutes or up to 20 minutes.

2 In a small bowl, mix the cornstarch with 2 tablespoons of the cream to make a slurry. Set aside.

3 In a saucepan, combine the remaining cream, the milk, sugar, corn syrup, bloomed saffron, cardamom, and salt and bring to a boil over medium heat, whisking constantly to dissolve the sugar. Add the cornstarch slurry and 6 of the gulab jamun balls and return to a boil, stirring continuously. Do not worry about the balls breaking up; the mixture will be blended. Boil, stirring continuously, for 3 minutes, then remove from the heat. Let cool slightly, then stir in the rose water.

4 Let the mixture cool to the touch, then transfer to a blender and blend until smooth, about 1 minute. Let cool to room temperature, add the rose water, then transfer to a container, cover tightly, and refrigerate for at least 4 hours or up to overnight.

5 Remove the chilled base from the refrigerator and stir to recombine. Transfer the base to your ice cream maker and churn according to the manufacturer's instructions. While the ice cream is churning, chop the remaining 4 gulab jamun balls into 1-inch pieces. Once the mixture has frozen to a soft consistency, using a rubber spatula, fold in the gulab jamun pieces. Serve the soft ice cream right away, or place in the freezer to freeze completely.

POOJA'S TIP

Gulab jamun is sold in cans; find it online and in Indian grocery stores.

Kheer Ice Cream

Kheer is the South Asian version of rice pudding. Every subculture—indeed, every family—makes it differently. My family's kheer is very milky, the rice is extremely overcooked and soft, and the only spice used is nutmeg. And that's exactly how I like it. In ice cream form, kheer is glorious—lightly spiced ice cream with bits of soft rice to break up the creaminess. There is nothing like it. This ice cream can be easily modified to incorporate whatever spice you like in your rice pudding.

MAKES 1 QUART

2 cups cooled cooked basmati rice

1 cup granulated cane sugar

½ cup whole milk

¾ teaspoon freshly grated nutmeg

1 cup heavy cream

¼ cup sweetened condensed milk

1 In a blender, combine 1¾ cups of the rice, the sugar, whole milk, and nutmeg and blend until a thick, smooth paste forms, about 2 minutes.

2 In a large bowl, using an electric mixer, beat the cream on high speed until stiff peaks form, about 3 minutes. Using a rubber spatula, fold in the condensed milk until well incorporated. Then fold in the rice mixture and the remaining ¼ cup rice until well mixed.

3 Transfer the mixture to a freezer-safe storage container and freeze for at least 4 hours or up to overnight before serving.

Ras Malai Ice Cream

Ras malai is a tricky dessert to make and an even trickier ice cream to make! At Malai, we use the best paneer we can find (looking at you, Sach Foods!), poach it in a simple syrup, drain it, and then heat it again with our ice cream base. It takes time and work, but produces a delicious ice cream that tastes like the dessert in frozen form. To simplify the process here, I make a ricotta ice cream—not exactly paneer, but close—to get a version that is still indulgent and delicious.

MAKES 1½ QUARTS

½ teaspoon packed saffron threads

¼ cup boiling water

3 tablespoons cream cheese, at room temperature

1 cup whole milk

1 cup heavy cream

¾ cup granulated cane sugar

2 tablespoons light corn syrup

½ teaspoon salt

1 teaspoon ground cardamom

1½ cups whole-milk ricotta cheese

¼ cup chopped pistachios

❶ To bloom the saffron, crush the saffron threads with your fingers and drop them into a small heatproof bowl. Add the boiling water and let sit to develop the flavor, at least 5 minutes or up to 20 minutes.

❷ In a large bowl, use an electric mixer, beat together the cream cheese, milk, cream, sugar, corn syrup, salt, bloomed saffron, and cardamom on medium speed until all the ingredients are well incorporated, about 3 minutes. Using a rubber spatula, fold in the ricotta cheese, mixing well.

❸ Transfer the mixture to your ice cream maker and churn according to the manufacturer's instructions. Serve the soft ice cream right away, or place in the freezer to freeze completely. Top with the pistachios just before serving.

Apple Pie Ice Cream

Many things remind me of my grandmother Ba, but none more than apple pie. She loved it all—the tanginess of the spiced apples with the buttery crust—and she would often make it as a special treat for the family. As the years went by, the frequency of the apple pie making decreased, resulting in my family taking Nutri-Grain Apple Cinnamon bars to India for Ba—right up until the last time we saw her. Man, she really loved her apple pie— in every form. I have no doubt that she would have loved this ice cream too.

MAKES 1½ QUARTS

FOR THE ICE CREAM BASE

1 tablespoon cornstarch

1¼ cups plus 2 tablespoons heavy cream

2 cups whole milk

3 cinnamon sticks

1 cup packed light brown sugar

¼ teaspoon salt

FOR THE APPLE INCLUSION

1 tablespoon unsalted butter

2 apples (preferably Fuji), peeled, cored, and cut into ½-inch pieces

2 tablespoons packed light brown sugar

Juice of ½ lemon

½ teaspoon ground cinnamon

½ teaspoon ground cardamom

¼ teaspoon ground allspice

Pinch of salt

4 Cardamom Snickerdoodles (page 167), roughly chopped

❶ To make the ice cream base, in a small bowl, mix the cornstarch with 2 tablespoons of the cream to make a slurry. Set aside.

❷ In a saucepan, combine the remaining 1¼ cups cream, the milk, cinnamon sticks, sugar, and salt and bring to a boil over medium heat, whisking constantly to dissolve the sugar. Continue to boil, whisking constantly, until everything is well incorporated, about 4 minutes. Reduce the heat to low and whisk in the cornstarch slurry, mixing well. Raise the heat to medium, bring to a boil, and boil, stirring, until slightly thickened, about 1 minute. Remove from the heat and let cool to room temperature.

❸ Strain the cooled base through a fine-mesh sieve into a container, cover tightly, and refrigerate for at least 4 hours. (If you have the time, letting it sit in the refrigerator overnight is ideal.)

❹ Meanwhile, prepare the apple inclusion. In a frying pan, melt the butter over medium-high heat. Add the apples and cook, stirring occasionally, until softened and coated with the butter, about 3 minutes. Add the sugar, lemon juice, ground cinnamon, cardamom, allspice, and salt and continue to cook, stirring occasionally, until the apples are tender and the liquid has evaporated, about 10 minutes. Remove from the heat and let cool completely. Transfer to an airtight container and keep at room temperature until ready to use.

❺ Remove the chilled base from the refrigerator and stir to recombine. Transfer the base to your ice cream maker and churn according to the manufacturer's instructions, adding the cooled apple mixture and ½ cup of the chopped snickerdoodles during the last 5 minutes of churning. Serve the soft ice cream right away, or place in the freezer to freeze completely.

Orange Creamsicle Mango Dolly Ice Cream

Mango Dolly is India's version of the Creamsicle. Both desserts have taken up space in my memory bank: eating a Dolly after playing cricket with my cousins in Ahmedabad, or having a Creamsicle after playing in the sprinkler in our backyard in Pennsylvania. They're essentially the same: vanilla ice cream surrounded by either mango or orange sherbet. Because making them can be a little complicated, I've not only fashioned them into a cohesive ice cream here but also combined the two flavors. The memories may be separate, but the feeling I had when eating them was the same.

MAKES 1 QUART

⅔ cup granulated cane sugar

Grated zest of 2 oranges

1 cup mango juice or mango purée (see Pooja's Tip)

1 cup sour cream

½ cup heavy cream

½ cup whole milk

2 tablespoons honey

2 teaspoons vanilla bean paste

1 In a small bowl, stir together the sugar and orange zest. Using your fingers, rub the orange zest into the sugar, coating the sugar well and releasing the essential oils in the zest.

2 In a blender, combine the zest-sugar mixture, mango juice, sour cream, heavy cream, milk, honey, and vanilla paste and blend until smooth, about 1½ minutes. Transfer to a container, cover tightly, and refrigerate for at least 2 hours or up to overnight.

3 Remove the chilled base from the refrigerator and stir to recombine. Transfer the base to your ice cream maker and churn according to the manufacturer's instructions. Serve the soft ice cream right away, or place in the freezer to freeze completely.

POOJA'S TIP

For the best result, look for mango juice or purée with no added sugar.

Dairy-Free Ice Cream
& Frozen Treats

Pineapple Pink Peppercorn Ice Cream

There are some ice cream flavors I conceptualize for Malai that I just know will be a hit. And there are other flavors that I'm a bit unsure about. This is one of them. Early on at Malai, after spending a few years developing our much-loved dairy-based ice creams, we started experimenting with dairy-free. It required a calculated balance between the coconut base and the ingredients that flavored it, and our experiments did not always work out. Here we have the obvious combination of pineapple and coconut but with the sharp yet fruity bite of pink peppercorn. We didn't think it would make it past its initial launch, but years later, it's our most popular dairy-free flavor!

MAKES 2 QUARTS

2½ cups coconut milk

2½ cups pineapple juice

1¼ cups granulated cane sugar

½ cup light corn syrup

2 teaspoons fresh lemon juice

¼ teaspoon salt

2 teaspoons pink peppercorns, coarsely crushed in a spice grinder or a mortar and pestle

1. In a saucepan, combine the coconut milk, pineapple juice, sugar, corn syrup, lemon juice, and salt and heat over medium heat, whisking occasionally, until everything is melted and well incorporated. Do not bring to a boil. Once the mixture is homogeneous, remove from the heat and let cool to room temperature.

2. Add the pink peppercorns and stir to combine. Transfer the cooled base to your ice cream maker and churn according to the manufacturer's instructions. Serve the soft ice cream right away, or place in the freezer to freeze completely.

MALAI FUN FACT

Despite the seemingly seasonal quality of this flavor, you can find pints of Pineapple Pink Peppercorn at Malai year-round because it's so popular!

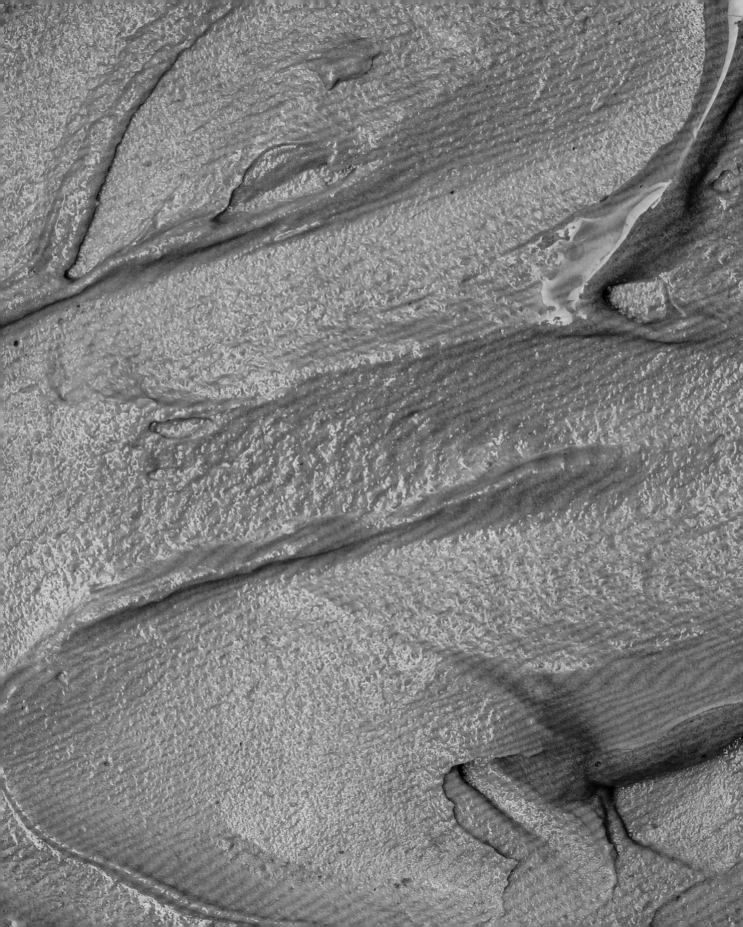

Hibiscus Chaat Masala Sorbet

In the Plum Sauce recipe on page 199, I tell the story of how my mom was once making a spiced plum juice that she left on the stove for too long, turning it into a thick sauce that we ended up pouring over vanilla ice cream. I created this sorbet as the frozen equivalent of that culinary mishap. I wanted to marry the umami saltiness of the chaat masala with the fruity sweetness of the plum, but I also wanted a flavor that was available year-round. Enter, hibiscus tea. It's acidic but not too much, has floral notes, and can be easily sweetened, making it the perfect balance to the spices.

MAKES 2 QUARTS

4¼ cups water

2 cups loose hibiscus flower tea or dried hibiscus flowers

1 cup granulated cane sugar

1½ teaspoons cornstarch

1 teaspoon chaat masala (see Pooja's Tip)

½ teaspoon salt

¾ cup light corn syrup

2 teaspoons fresh lemon juice

❶ In a saucepan, bring the water to a boil over medium heat. Add the hibiscus, reduce the heat to medium-low, and simmer the tea for 20 minutes.

❷ Remove from the heat and let the tea steep for another 20 minutes. Strain the tea through a fine-mesh sieve into a medium bowl. Make sure to press against the solids in the sieve to release as much moisture as possible.

❸ In a small bowl, whisk together the sugar, cornstarch, chaat masala, and salt, mixing well. Whisk the sugar mixture into the hibiscus tea until fully dissolved. Then whisk in the corn syrup and lemon juice until well incorporated.

❹ Let the mixture cool to room temperature. Transfer the mixture to your ice cream maker and churn according to the manufacturer's instructions. Serve the soft sorbet right away, or place in the freezer to freeze completely.

POOJA'S TIP

Chaat masala is an umami blend of spices that typically consists of dry mango powder, cumin, coriander, black salt, and chili powder. It is great on a lot of things but especially on fruit, which is why it works so well here. You can find chaat masala in Indian grocery stores and online.

Spiced Peanut Crunch Ice Cream

I *love* peanut butter ice cream. When I was little, my family would often go to TCBY, and I would get a parfait with golden vanilla yogurt, peanut butter sauce, chocolate sauce, peanut butter cups, and peanut butter candies. This order has been fact-checked by my family. Even now, if I go out for ice cream (that's not Malai, of course), I almost always opt for something peanut buttery. So obviously I had to create a peanut butter ice cream for Malai. It's basically Peanut Chikki (page 196) in ice cream form with a little spice, a touch of heat, and no dairy.

MAKES 1½ QUARTS

2½ cups coconut milk

½ cup granulated cane sugar

2 tablespoons light corn syrup

⅓ cup creamy natural peanut butter

½ teaspoon ground star anise

¼ teaspoon salt

⅛ teaspoon cayenne pepper

⅓ cup chopped raw peanuts

1. In a saucepan, combine the coconut milk, sugar, corn syrup, peanut butter, star anise, salt, and cayenne pepper and heat over medium heat, whisking occasionally, until everything is melted and well incorporated. Do not bring to a boil. Once the mixture is homogeneous, remove from the heat and let cool to room temperature.

2. Transfer the cooled base to your ice cream maker and churn according to the manufacturer's instructions, adding the peanuts during the last 5 minutes of churning. Serve the soft ice cream right away, or place in the freezer to freeze completely.

POOJA'S TIP

To grind star anise, place a few in a spice or coffee grinder and pulse until a fine powder. You can store leftover ground star anise in an airtight container.

Sweet Corn Saffron Ice Cream

This is a summer seasonal flavor at Malai, and it's one of the most anticipated. Pairing sweet summer corn with the honey-like notes of saffron yields an ice cream that is out of this world—in this case, one that's dairy-free. The coconut plays off the corn and saffron beautifully, and it makes the whole thing taste like a vacation. For some peak-summer decadence, top it with Blueberry Cardamom Sauce (page 203).

MAKES 1 QUART

½ teaspoon packed saffron threads

2 tablespoons boiling water

2 ears corn, shucked and silk removed

1 can (15 ounces) coconut milk

⅓ cup granulated cane sugar

2 tablespoons light corn syrup

¼ teaspoon salt

1. To bloom the saffron, crush the saffron threads with your fingers and drop them into a small heatproof bowl. Add the boiling water and let sit to develop the flavor, at least 5 minutes or up to 20 minutes.

2. Cut enough kernels from the corn ears to yield 1 cup. Be sure to scrape the cobs with the back of the knife to get all the milky juice and tender pulp, which have lots of corn flavor.

3. In a saucepan, combine the corn, coconut milk, sugar, corn syrup, bloomed saffron, and salt and bring to a boil over medium-high heat, whisking constantly to dissolve the sugar. Once a boil is reached, remove from the heat and let cool to room temperature.

4. Transfer the cooled mixture to a blender and blend until smooth, about 1 minute. Pour into a container, cover tightly, and refrigerate until well chilled, about 4 hours.

5. Remove the chilled base from the refrigerator and stir to recombine. Transfer the base to your ice cream maker and churn according to the manufacturer's instructions. Serve the soft ice cream right away, or place in the freezer to freeze completely.

Lychee Rose Water Sorbet

It is hard not to love lychees. They boast a range of flavors—sweet, tangy, and floral—and are available for such a short season that you want to savor them every minute of it. Sorbet is a perfect way to showcase this tropical fruit, as there are no ingredients such as dairy or coconut to mask its unique taste. The addition of rose water makes this frozen treat super special. Top off this sorbet with a bubbly beverage—alcoholic or not—for the most refreshing summertime drink!

MAKES 1½ QUARTS

1½ cups water

1 cup granulated cane sugar

⅓ cup light corn syrup

½ teaspoon cornstarch

1 cup lychee purée
(see Pooja's Tip)

¼ cup rose water

1 tablespoon fresh lemon juice

1 In a saucepan, combine the water, sugar, corn syrup, and cornstarch and heat over medium heat, stirring constantly, until the sugar dissolves and everything is well incorporated, 3–4 minutes. Remove from the heat and let cool to room temperature.

2 Add the lychee purée, rose water, and lemon juice to the cooled mixture and stir to combine. Transfer the mixture to your ice cream maker and churn according to the manufacturer's instructions. Serve the soft sorbet right away, or place in the freezer to freeze completely.

POOJA'S TIP

Fruit purées are readily available online. Look for a lychee purée that doesn't have any added sugar. I like to use purchased unsweetened fruit purées, instead of making my own, to ensure consistency and availability of flavors any time of year.

Passion Fruit Cilantro Sorbet

I made a confession about cardamom on page 144, and I have the same confession about cilantro—except it's weirder. I love the flavor of *blended* cilantro. Put a cilantro chutney in front of me, and I couldn't be happier. But cilantro leaves? I'm out. It's the taste not the texture—and, yes, I'm aware that it's strange. Here, cilantro leaves are blended into a passion fruit sorbet and the result is a flavor explosion of all things good. The mix of the bright, tart notes of passion fruit with the grassiness of (blended) cilantro is refreshing and delightful.

MAKES 1½ QUARTS

1½ cups water

1 cup granulated cane sugar

¼ cup light corn syrup

½ teaspoon cornstarch

1 cup passion fruit purée

¼ cup fresh cilantro leaves

1 tablespoon fresh lemon juice

❶ In a saucepan, combine the water, sugar, corn syrup, and cornstarch and heat over medium heat, stirring constantly, until the sugar dissolves and everything is well incorporated. 3–4 minutes. Remove from the heat and let cool to room temperature.

❷ Add the passion fruit purée, cilantro, and lemon juice to the cooled mixture and stir to mix well. Transfer the mixture to a blender and blend on high speed until smooth, 1–2 minutes. Strain through a fine-mesh sieve into a bowl to to remove any remaining cilantro leaf bits.

❸ Transfer the mixture to your ice cream maker and churn according to the manufacturer's instructions. Serve the soft sorbet right away, or place in the freezer to freeze completely.

Chocolate Clove Ice Cream

One of our seasonal soft-serve flavors at Malai is chocolate scented with clove. I remember a customer trying it and remarking on how "clovey" it tasted. He then followed that up with, "That's cool!" You know what? Cloves *are* cool. They get a bad rap for being too strong and overbearing and for having a spicy bitterness that is unlike any of the warming spices. But those flavor notes pair beautifully with chocolate. After having this you, too, will learn to embrace the clove.

MAKES 1 QUART

1 can (15 ounces) coconut milk

¾ cup water

⅔ cup unsweetened natural cocoa powder

⅔ cup granulated cane sugar

2 tablespoons light corn syrup

¼ teaspoon ground cloves

1 In a saucepan, whisk together the coconut milk, water, cocoa powder, sugar, corn syrup, and cloves. Place over medium heat and heat, stirring constantly, until the sugar dissolves, everything is well incorporated, and no lumps remain, 4–5 minutes. Remove from the heat and transfer to a heatproof container.

2 Let the base cool to room temperature, then cover tightly and refrigerate until well chilled, about 4 hours.

3 Remove the chilled base from the refrigerator and stir to recombine. Transfer the chilled base to your ice cream maker and churn according to the manufacturer's instructions. Serve the soft ice cream right away, or place in the freezer to freeze completely.

Coconut Date Garam Masala Ice Cream

Sticky toffee pudding is one of my favorite desserts to make (and actually was the dessert I paired that first Ginger and Star Anise ice creams, pages 35 and 36, with during the fateful Friendsgiving!), and this ice cream has sticky toffee pudding vibes. Jammy dates, cooling coconut, and the warmth of sweet garam masala—if there ever was a contest for the ultimate cozy ice cream, this would win it.

MAKES 1½ QUARTS

FOR THE DATE CARAMEL

6 Medjool dates, pitted

½ cup boiling water

2 tablespoons coconut oil

1½ teaspoons garam masala
(see Pantry Staples, page 19)

¼ teaspoon salt

¼ cup cold water

FOR THE ICE CREAM

2 cans (15 ounces each)
coconut milk

⅔ cup granulated cane sugar

2 tablespoons grade A
maple syrup

2 tablespoons coconut oil

2 tablespoons cocoa butter

¼ teaspoon salt

1 To make the date caramel, in a heatproof bowl, combine the dates and boiling water and let sit for 10 minutes. Drain the dates and add them to a high-speed blender along with the coconut oil, garam masala, salt, and cold water. Blend until the mixture is smooth and has the consistency of a thick caramel sauce, about 3 minutes. Set aside.

2 To make the ice cream, in a saucepan, combine the coconut milk, sugar, maple syrup, coconut oil, cocoa butter, and salt and heat over medium heat, whisking constantly, until the sugar dissolves, the cocoa butter breaks down, and the mixture is homogeneous, about 5 minutes. Remove from the heat and let cool to room temperature.

3 Transfer the cooled base to your ice cream maker and churn according to the manufacturer's instructions, adding the date caramel during the last 5 minutes of churning. Serve the soft ice cream right away, or place in the freezer to freeze completely.

Coffee Jaggery Ice Cream

This ice cream flavor may not sound all that exciting, but sometimes you just need a solid product made of a few high-quality ingredients for a flavor to shine. The molasses notes of the jaggery pair brilliantly with the bitter, chocolaty notes of the coffee. All of that plus cooling coconut and this ice cream becomes capable of stealing the spotlight from its fellow ice creams.

MAKES 1 QUART

1 can (13.5 ounces) coconut cream

1 can (15 ounces) coconut milk

½ cup powdered jaggery (see Pooja's Tip, page 41)

¼ cup light corn syrup

1 teaspoon tapioca starch

¼ cup coffee beans

1 tablespoon vodka (see Pooja's Tip, page 63)

1 In a saucepan, combine the coconut cream, coconut milk, jaggery, corn syrup, and tapioca starch and heat over medium-high heat, stirring constantly, until the jaggery melts, everything is well incorporated, and the mixture is homogeneous, about 5 minutes. Remove from the heat and add the coffee beans and vodka. Let the mixture steep for 30 minutes.

2 Strain the mixture through a fine-mesh sieve into a container, let cool to room temperature, cover tightly, and refrigerate until well chilled, about 4 hours.

3 Remove the chilled base from the refrigerator and stir to recombine. Transfer the chilled base to your ice cream maker and churn according to the manufacturer's instructions. Serve the soft ice cream right away, or place in the freezer to freeze completely.

Nimbu Pani Sorbet

Nimbu pani, exactly translating to "lemon water," is the Indian version of lemonade. It is a mixture of lemon juice, lime juice, water, sugar, salt, and spices—usually something umami like black salt or chaat masala. More than anything, it's wildly thirst quenching and refreshing. Our family would often travel to India in the summer, and during those hot, humid days when we would go from house to house to visit various members of our extended family, we would always be presented with a cold glass of nimbu pani. I loved visiting family, but I secretly loved the nimbu pani more. It was cool, tart, and sweet enough to hold me over until the next visit of the day. This sorbet version has all the same flavors in frozen form—the perfect cure for a hot day.

MAKES 1½ QUARTS

1¾ cups water

2 cups granulated cane sugar

2 cups fresh lemon juice

1 teaspoon chaat masala
(see Pooja's Tip, page 87)

½ teaspoon black salt
(see Pooja's Tip)

1 In a saucepan, combine the water and sugar and bring to a boil over medium-high heat, stirring constantly, until the sugar dissolves, 3–4 minutes. Remove from the heat and stir in the lemon juice, chaat masala, and black salt. Let cool to room temperature.

2 Transfer the cooled mixture to your ice cream maker and churn according to the manufacturer's instructions. Serve the soft sorbet right away, or place in the freezer to freeze completely.

POOJA'S TIP

Black salt, known as kala namak, is a rock salt mined in the mountainous areas of northern India and surrounding countries. It has a pungent, umami-like (sulfur) flavor. Look for it in Indian grocery stores and online.

Cinnamon Water Sorbet

Welcome drinks are their own category in Indian culture. When you go to someone's home or host someone at yours, there is always some sort of special drink that is served in addition to more common beverages. Welcome drinks inspired recipes in this book like the Cold Coffee Milkshake (page 127) and the Plum Sauce (page 199). But there was one welcome drink that my aunt made once that intrigued me. It was a cinnamony, spicy, slightly sweetened beverage that blew me away. When I asked her what it was, her response was simply "cinnamon water." I got the recipe from her and turned the drink into a sorbet. And I can assure you that the end result is much more complex and delicious than its plain name suggests.

MAKES 2 QUARTS

1½ cups granulated
cane sugar

½ teaspoon cornstarch

¼ cup light corn syrup

3 cups water

3 cinnamon sticks

4 whole cloves

5 black peppercorns

2 tablespoons fresh
lemon juice

1 In a saucepan, combine 1 cup of the sugar, the cornstarch, corn syrup, and 1½ cups of the water and heat over medium heat, stirring constantly, until the sugar dissolves, 3–4 minutes. Remove from the heat and let cool to room temperature.

2 Meanwhile, in a second saucepan, combine the remaining 1½ cups water, the remaining ½ cup sugar, the cinnamon, cloves, and peppercorns and bring to a boil over medium-high heat, stirring constantly to dissolve the sugar. Continue to boil for 2 minutes, then remove from the heat. Stir in the lemon juice and let cool to room temperature. Strain the cooled spice water through a fine-mesh sieve into a bowl and discard the solids.

3 Add the cooled sorbet base to the spice water and stir to mix. Transfer the mixture to your ice cream maker and churn according to the manufacturer's instructions. Serve the soft sorbet right away, or place in the freezer to freeze completely.

Kachi Keri Granita

One of the stories from her childhood that my mom told me long ago was about eating baraf no golo—basically a mix between a snow cone and shaved ice. In the evening after dinner, she and her family would venture out to find a street vendor who would compact soft ice shavings into a bowl and then flavor them with whatever fresh fruit syrups were on hand. She said that her go-to syrup choice was always kachi keri, or unripe mango. A common ingredient in India, kachi keri has the distinct flavor of mango but without the sugariness of a ripe mango. It has a pleasing acidity with a mild sweetness. When I finally had a chance to try it myself, it met all my high expectations, and it turned out that kachi keri was my favorite syrup flavor too. This is as close as I can get to that Indian street-vendor experience in the States. It's not the same, but it's just as good!

MAKES 1½ QUARTS

2 cups cubed, unripe frozen mango (see Pooja's Tip)

2 tablespoons fresh lemon juice

¼ cup granulated cane sugar

⅛ teaspoon kosher salt

❶ In a blender, combine the mango, lemon juice, sugar, and salt and blend to a smooth purée, about 1 minute.

❷ Pour the purée into an 8-inch square freezer-safe pan and place in the freezer for 30 minutes. Remove the pan from the freezer and scrape the partially frozen mixture with the tines of a fork, breaking up any large clumps. Return the pan to the freezer for another 30 minutes, then remove it and again scrape the mixture with the fork tines. Repeat this process every 30 minutes for a total of 4 hours.

❸ The granita is ready when the mixture is completely frozen and has a uniformly dry, flaky texture. Serve right away.

POOJA'S TIP

You can find fresh and frozen unripe mango, also known as green mango, in Indian grocery stores. If using unpeeled fresh mango, be sure to peel it before using in this recipe.

Magic Banana Ginger Ice Cream

This ice cream is actually the first one I ever made. I found out, during those early years of living alone, that making banana bread was not your only choice when you are rich in overripe bananas. You can also freeze them and turn them into banana ice cream. I have done an endless combination of this easy banana ice cream: Nutella and tea biscuits; peanut butter and graham crackers; plain with chocolate chips. But this cashew-ginger version elevates this ice cream from a weeknight snack to a proper dessert—and just as easy.

MAKES 2 CUPS

4 overripe bananas, peeled, cut into 1-inch pieces, and frozen overnight

⅓ cup cashew butter

2 tablespoons agave nectar or honey

2 tablespoons plant-based milk

½ teaspoon ground ginger

¼ teaspoon salt

❶ Add the bananas to a food processor or blender and process until the consistency of soft-serve ice cream, stopping to scrape down the sides of the bowl or beaker with a rubber spatula if needed. Add the cashew butter, agave nectar, milk, ginger, and salt and process until smooth, about 1 minute. Serve right away.

Coconut Saffron Kulfi Ice Pops

My vegan cousin does a lot of our initial taste testing for Malai's dairy-free treats. He's not the most effusive guy, so getting him to gush is out of the question. Even getting a thumbs-up is difficult. When he said that these ice pops were "very good," I nearly lost it and then immediately placed them on the menu. I agree, they are very good.

MAKES 8–10 ICE POPS

½ teaspoon packed saffron threads

2 tablespoons boiling water

1½ cups coconut milk

1 can (15 ounces) condensed coconut milk

1 can (15 ounces) evaporated coconut milk

¼ teaspoon salt

❶ To bloom the saffron, crush the saffron threads with your fingers and drop them into a small heatproof bowl. Add the boiling water and let sit to develop the flavor, at least 5 minutes or up to 20 minutes.

❷ In a bowl, combine the coconut milk, condensed coconut milk, evaporated coconut milk, and salt. Add the bloomed saffron and whisk to mix everything well.

❸ Divide the mixture evenly among 8–10 ice-pop molds and freeze for at least 6 hours or up to overnight before serving.

Tulsi Tea & Dark Chocolate Granita

At Malai, I am often thinking about how I can take a popular dairy-based treat and turn it into an equally delicious and satisfying dairy-free one. Our Tulsi Chocolate Chip—our version of mint chocolate chip but using tulsi, or holy basil, instead of mint—is one of my favorite flavors, so I knew I had to create a dairy-free version. The result is tulsi tea–flavored granita, finished with a ribbon of melted chocolate and a dollop of whipped coconut cream. It's not an exact replica of the dairy ice cream, but it checks off both delicious and satisfying.

MAKES 1½ QUARTS

1 cup brewed tulsi tea, at room temperature

3 tablespoons granulated cane sugar

1 tablespoon fresh lemon juice

⅛ teaspoon salt

Melted dark chocolate, for serving

Whipped coconut cream, for serving

1 In a blender, combine the tea, sugar, lemon juice, and salt and blend until smooth, about 1 minute.

2 Pour the mixture into an 8-inch square freezer-safe pan and place in the freezer for 30 minutes. Remove the pan from the freezer and scrape the partially frozen mixture with the tines of a fork, breaking up any large clumps. Return the pan to the freezer for another 30 minutes, then remove it and again scrape the mixture with the fork tines. Repeat this process every 30 minutes for a total of 4 hours.

3 The granita is ready when the mixture is completely frozen and has a uniformly dry, flaky texture. Serve right away, topping each serving with a drizzle of dark chocolate and a dollop of whipped coconut cream.

Ice Cream Desserts

Strawberry Rose Ice Cream Float

I never really understood the appeal of soda floats. Why would anyone want a delicious and creamy scoop of ice cream in...water?! But when I was challenged to make a float recipe, I came to understand that it was so much more. The effervescence of the carbonation combined with a delicious syrup are what make floats so exciting, light, and refreshing. I've really come around on floats—they're great!

MAKES 2 ICE CREAM FLOATS

FOR THE SYRUP

1 cup hulled and quartered strawberries

1½ tablespoons granulated cane sugar

2 tablespoons water

1½ tablespoons fresh lemon juice

2 teaspoons rose water

2 cans (12 ounces each) seltzer water

4 scoops ice cream, any flavor

❶ To make the syrup, in a blender, combine the strawberries, sugar, water, lemon juice, and rose water and blend until smooth. Strain through a fine-mesh sieve into a bowl. The syrup can be made up to 1 day in advance and stored in an airtight container in the refrigerator until ready to use.

❷ To assemble a float, add 1–2 tablespoons of the syrup to a tall glass and top with about half of a can of the seltzer water. Drop in a scoop of ice cream and add 1–2 tablespoons of the syrup. Pour in the remaining seltzer from the can and add a second scoop of ice cream. Repeat with another glass to make a second float. Provide each float with a straw and a spoon and serve right away.

Dorie Greenspan's Pineapple Banana Split

I had never had a banana split—ever—until Dorie Greenspan entered my life. She is the dessert queen, having written the most amazing cookbooks without a single failing recipe, and when she makes a banana split, I eat a banana split. And the moment I did, I got it. It was sweet and fruity, creamy and crunchy. It wasn't too sweet, even though I thought it would be, and it was extremely satisfying, even though I didn't think it would be. This is the recipe that Dorie created when she collaborated with Malai. You will need to make the roasted pineapple, streusel, and ice cream in advance, so plan accordingly.

MAKES 6 BANANA SPLITS

FOR THE SPICED AND ROASTED PINEAPPLE

1 ripe pineapple

½ cup fresh orange juice

½ cup dark rum

1 jar (about 12 ounces) peach jam

1 vanilla bean, split lengthwise

¼ cup whole spices of choice, such as pink peppercorns, black peppercorns, coriander seeds, cinnamon stick, cardamom seeds, star anise, and/or bay leaves, lightly bruised

FOR THE STREUSEL CHUNKLETS

¾ cup all-purpose flour

3 tablespoons granulated cane sugar

1 tablespoon packed light brown sugar

¼ teaspoon ground cinnamon

¼ teaspoon fine sea salt

5½ tablespoons cold unsalted butter, cut into small cubes

½ teaspoon pure vanilla extract

① To make the roasted pineapple, preheat the oven to 300°F.

② Peel the pineapple, cut into quarters lengthwise, and slice away the core from each quarter. Arrange the pineapple quarters in a baking pan large enough to hold them without crowding (you need room to baste). In a bowl, whisk together the orange juice, rum, and jam, mixing well. Pour the mixture evenly over the pineapple and then toss the vanilla bean and spices into the pan, distributing them evenly.

③ Roast the pineapple, basting and turning the pieces in the syrup every 20 minutes or so, until it is tender and easily pierced with a knife, about 2 hours. The fruit will be candied. Let cool, then transfer the pineapple to a plate. Strain the syrup in the pan through a fine-mesh sieve into a bowl and discard the vanilla bean and spices. Cut the pineapple into sundae-size morsels. The pineapple and syrup can be made up to 1 day in advance. Store in separate airtight containers in the refrigerator.

④ To make the streusel chunklets, in the bowl of a stand mixer, whisk together the flour, granulated and brown sugars, cinnamon, and salt. Drop in the butter cubes and toss the ingredients together with your fingers until the butter is evenly coated with the flour mixture.

**FOR THE CARAMELIZED
BANANAS**

**6 tablespoons granulated
cane sugar**

**3 bananas, peeled and halved
lengthwise**

4 tablespoons unsalted butter

**Pineapple Pink Peppercorn
Ice Cream (page 84)**

**Spiced Whipped Cream
(page 204)**

5 Attach the bowl to the mixer stand, fit the mixer with the paddle attachment, and mix on medium-low speed until the ingredients form moist, clumpy crumbs. When you pinch the streusel, it should hold together. (Reaching this stage may take longer than you are expecting, so hold on and keep testing.) Sprinkle in the vanilla and mix just until blended. Cover and refrigerate for at least 1 hour or up to 3 hours.

6 Preheat the oven to 350°F. Line a sheet pan with parchment paper. Spread the streusel mixture over the prepared pan. (It should be clumpy. If it's not, pinch it to form it into clumps.) Bake the streusel, stirring often, until golden brown, 15–17 minutes. Let cool completely on the pan on a wire rack. Set aside until ready to assemble the banana splits.

7 Just before you are ready to assemble the banana splits, prepare the caramelized bananas. Pour the sugar onto a shallow plate. One at a time, dip the cut side of each banana half into the sugar to coat evenly and set aside, sugar side up.

8 In a large frying pan, melt the butter over medium heat. When the butter begins to foam, add the banana halves, sugar side down, and cook until the sugar has caramelized and the underside is golden brown, about 3 minutes. Transfer to a plate, sugar side up.

9 To assemble the banana splits, lay a banana half, caramelized side up, in each serving dish. Top with the pineapple pieces, dividing them evenly, then drizzle the pineapple with some of the syrup. Arrange scoops of the ice cream on top of the pineapple and sprinkle the ice cream with the streusel. Top with whipped cream and more syrup from the roasted pineapple and serve right away.

Chai Float

Considering how much my mom's masala chai is a part of Malai's origin story and, honestly, my origin story, you would think my mom would be proud that I created an ice cream flavor inspired by it. But no. Out of all the ice creams that we have developed at Malai throughout the years, Masala Chai is the only one that she will not enjoy. "Chai is not supposed to be cold," she says very bluntly. If you are one of the few in her camp, you can stop after straining the chai in this recipe and enjoy it warm. If you are anyone else, enjoy the chai with a scoop of ice cream for a hot and cold delight.

**MAKES 1 ICE CREAM
FLOAT**

---

1 cup water

1 tablespoon granulated
cane sugar

½ teaspoon Malai Chai
Masala (see Malai Fun Fact,
page 38)

1-inch piece fresh ginger,
peeled and minced

⅓ cup 2 percent milk

2–3 fresh mint leaves
(optional)

1 tablespoon loose CTC
black tea (see Pooja's Tip,
page 39)

1 scoop Masala Chai
Ice Cream (page 38)

1 In a small saucepan, warm the water over medium-high heat, then add the sugar, chai masala, and ginger and bring to a rolling boil. Add the milk and let warm through, then add the mint, if using. When the mixture just starts to boil, reduce the heat to medium and add the tea. Stir and let the mixture boil gently until it turns a golden amber, about 45 seconds.

2 Remove from the heat and strain the tea through a fine-mesh sieve or tea strainer into a mug. Add the ice cream and enjoy!

Crunchy Ice Cream Balls

This recipe is your answer to the quickest and most delicious dessert for a dinner party or a solo craving for something sweet. It has fried ice cream vibes, ice cream sundae energy, and an ice cream sandwich aura. Once you make these crunchy ice cream balls for the first time, I'm almost certain that you'll never stop.

MAKES 10–12 SERVINGS

1 pint ice cream, any flavor

4 digestive biscuits or graham crackers

2 tablespoons ghee or unsalted butter

¼ teaspoon ground cinnamon

Chocolate Cardamom Sauce (page 186), for serving

❶ Line a sheet pan with parchment paper. Using a small ice cream scoop or tablespoon, scoop out 1-ounce balls of ice cream and place them, not touching, on the prepared pan. (You'll have about 16 balls of ice cream.) Slip the pan into the freezer and freeze the balls until solid, about 4 hours.

❷ While the ice cream balls are freezing, crush the biscuits or graham crackers until coarsely ground. In a frying pan, heat 1 tablespoon of the ghee over medium heat. When the ghee has melted, add the crushed biscuits, reduce the heat to medium-low, and toast, stirring continuously, until golden brown, about 4 minutes. Remove from the heat, pour into a shallow bowl, and let cool completely. Set aside until needed. Wipe out the pan and reserve.

❸ When ready to assemble, add the remaining 1 tablespoon ghee to the reserved pan, melt over low heat, pour into a small heatproof bowl, and let cool. Remove the ice cream balls from the freezer. One at a time, coat them on all sides with the ghee, quickly roll them in the toasted crumbs, coating on all sides, and return them to the sheet pan.

❹ When all the balls are coated, serve immediately with the sauce or return them to the freezer for up to 4 hours before serving. Serve with the sauce on the side for dipping.

Orange Fennel French Toast

Best. Breakfast. Ever. And nothing that you say can convince me otherwise. Using melted ice cream as the custard base for French toast is not only all sorts of decadent but also introduces the flavor of the ice cream to the morning meal. We debuted this dish for National Ice Cream for Breakfast Day (the very best holiday), and it was so popular that we bring it back every year. You can go conventional on the topping— maple syrup, confectioners' sugar, whipped cream—but I like to finish my French toast with a scoop of Coffee Cardamom Ice Cream (page 37) and maybe even some Chocolate Cardamom Sauce (page 186).

MAKES 6 SERVINGS

---

2 pints Orange Fennel Ice Cream (page 45), melted

1 tablespoon cornstarch

6 slices brioche or challah bread, each about 1 inch thick

3 tablespoons unsalted butter

Maple syrup, whipped cream, confectioners' sugar, Chocolate Cardamom Sauce (page 186), or Coffee Cardamom Ice Cream (page 37), for serving

❶ Preheat the oven to 200°F. Pour the melted ice cream into a 9 x 13-inch baking pan and whisk in the cornstarch until well mixed. Lay the bread slices in a single layer on top of the ice cream and press down on them so the bread fully absorbs the ice cream. Let sit for 3–4 minutes. Flip the bread and let the other side soak for another 3–4 minutes.

❷ In a nonstick frying pan, melt ½ tablespoon of the butter over medium heat. When the butter is hot, using a spatula, carefully transfer a slice of the bread from the ice cream mixture, allowing the excess ice cream to drip off, to the hot pan. Fry until the first side is golden brown, about 3 minutes, adjusting the heat as necessary to make sure the bread does not burn. Flip the bread with the spatula and fry on the second side until golden brown, about 3 minutes longer.

❸ Transfer the toasted bread to a sheet pan or ovenproof platter and place in the oven to keep warm. Repeat with the remaining soaked bread slices and butter.

❹ Serve the French toast right away with the topping of your choice.

Jaggery Cones

I almost didn't include this recipe in the book. Who has a waffle cone maker? Who has a cone mold? Who is going to source the ingredients for this very specific cone recipe? The thing is, the cones are just that good. They are perfectly crisp and sweet and have that deep flavor of jaggery. They are worth the cone maker and the mold and getting the ingredients. (But if you don't have those things, you can also make them in a frying pan.) And they are worth it because they are used in the recipe directly after this, Malai Drumsticks (page 124). Try them both, and I'm positive you'll agree with me.

MAKES 8 CONES

5 tablespoons powdered jaggery (see Pooja's Tip, page 41)

1 tablespoon granulated cane sugar

½ teaspoon cornstarch

⅛ teaspoon salt

1½ tablespoons unsalted butter, at room temperature

2 tablespoons water

⅔ cup all-purpose flour

½ teaspoon baking powder

Neutral oil, such as grapeseed, for brushing the waffle cone maker

1 In a saucepan, whisk together the jaggery, sugar, cornstarch, salt, butter, and water, mixing well. Place over medium heat and whisk constantly until thickened, 2–3 minutes. Remove from the heat and whisk in the flour and baking powder until smooth. The batter should be free flowing and have the consistency of pancake batter. Add a little water if needed.

2 Following the manufacturer's instructions, preheat the waffle cone maker to a color setting of around 4. Lightly brush both grids with oil.

3 Spoon 2 tablespoons of the batter onto the center of the bottom grid, close the lid, and bake for about 1½ minutes. Open the maker, then, with a fork, carefully lift the waffle from the grid. Using a clean dish towel to protect your fingers from the heat, roll the waffle around the cone mold, pinching the bottom, and hold the cone for about 10 seconds to ensure it keeps its shape. Slide the cone free of the mold and set aside to cool completely. Repeat with the remaining batter.

4 The cones will keep in an airtight container at room temperature for up to 1 week.

POOJA'S TIP

If you don't have a waffle cone maker but you do have a waffle cone mold, you can still make the cones. Heat a frying pan over medium-high heat and lightly brush the bottom with a neutral oil. Spoon 2 tablespoons of the batter onto the pan and, using the back of wooden spoon, spread in a thin circle about 4 inches in diameter. Let it fry until light brown on the underside, about 1½ minutes. Flip and cook on the second side until light brown, about 1½ minutes longer. Shape the cone around the cone mold as directed. This won't create as thin or as crisp a cone, but the cones will still be tasty. And if you don't have a cone mold, you can shape the cones into a bowl to make waffle bowls!

Malai Drumsticks

This recipe is both very easy and very labor intensive. If you already have all the ingredients on hand—homemade cones, ice cream, sauce, topping—this is a cinch to put together. If you don't, this recipe becomes quite a process. But I will leave you with this story: During the first part of the pandemic, when New York City was on complete lockdown, my sister and I made tons of these little drumsticks and ate one every single day. Making them was a labor of love, but that daily ritual of eating one with my sister is still one of my favorite memories from that time.

MAKES 6 DRUMSTICKS

---

6 Jaggery Cones (page 123)

1 batch Magic Shell (page 200)

1½ quarts Spiced Peanut Crunch Ice Cream (page 88)

½ cup Peanut Chikki (page 196)

❶ Place 6 short glasses in a 9 x 13-inch baking pan. Place a jaggery cone in each glass. Make sure the top edge of each cone is at least 2 inches taller than the glass rim.

❷ Pour 1 tablespoon of the Magic Shell into the bottom of each cone. Using a spoon, pack the ice cream inside the cones, making sure it touches the sauce on the bottom of the cone and forms a domed scoop on top. Place the filled cones in the freezer for 15 minutes.

❸ Pour the remaining Magic Shell into a small, deep bowl or glass wide enough to accommodate a filled cone. Pour the Peanut Chikki into a shallow bowl. Remove the cones from the freezer. Turn a cone upside down and dip it into the Magic Shell to cover the domed ice cream scoop on top. Immediately, before the shell hardens, roll the top of the cone in the Peanut Chikki, coating the shell, and then set the cone back into its glass. Repeat with each of the cones.

❹ Once all the cones are dipped and coated, return them to the freezer to harden, about 30 minutes. Remove from the freezer and enjoy!

MALAI FUN FACT

We made these cones with our Spiced Peanut Butter Crunch Ice Cream for our one-year anniversary party of our flagship store in Brooklyn, and they were a hit! We've constantly talked about when we should bring them back—and maybe one day we will.

Cold Coffee Milkshake

Cold coffee is its own culture in India. It's a treat that you crave at night when you're going for a drive as the warm day is just beginning to cool off. It's a midmorning pick-me-up when you feel like having something indulgent; and it's the ideal drink to treat unexpected guests. The version I grew up with has a milky sweet coffee flavor and the decadence of a milkshake. It's easy to whip together, and it's perfect every time.

MAKES 2 MILKSHAKES

¼ cup Chocolate Cardamom Sauce (page 186)

2 tablespoons warm water

1½ tablespoons instant coffee powder

2 tablespoons granulated cane sugar

1¾ cups milk, any type except skim

1 scoop ice cream, any flavor

❶ Using 2 sundae glasses or tall float glasses, drizzle the chocolate sauce down along the sides. Place in the refrigerator until the rest of the components are ready.

❷ In a blender, combine the water, coffee powder, and sugar and blend on high speed until the mixture is frothy and the sugar and coffee are completely dissolved. Add the milk and ice cream and blend until smooth.

❸ Pour into the prepared glasses and serve cold.

Falooda Sundae

In the early days of Malai, I was trying to sell at as many New York City summer street fairs as possible. Back then, the most important day of the year was always National Ice Cream Day in July. It would draw the most number of people, as well as press. In those years, I was nervous about whether our flavors would resonate with wider audiences, but that did not make me any less bold. One year for National Ice Cream Day, I decided we should make falooda sundaes. They were a riff on the popular cold drink of the same name made with milk, rose syrup, a scoop of ice cream, crunchy, dense basil seeds, and chewy vermicelli noodles—yes, there's a lot going on, but it all works together perfectly. It was a bit risky, but I wanted to introduce the wonders of falooda through our sundae. I still remember the joy we felt when, at the end of that weekend, there were press mentions of how our falooda sundaes took the best in show prize.

MAKES 4 SUNDAES

¼ cup rose syrup (see Pooja's Tip)

2 tablespoons pomegranate molasses (see Pooja's Tip)

1 tablespoon sweet basil seeds (see Pooja's Tip)

½ cup water

½ cup prepared falooda sev (see Pooja's Tip)

4 scoops Sweet Milk Ice Cream (page 31)

Pomegranate seeds, for garnish

❶ In a small bowl, stir together the rose syrup and pomegranate molasses and set aside.

❷ In a second small bowl, add the basil seeds to the water and let soak for 20 minutes. They will bloom and soak up the water. Drain off any residual water and set the seeds aside.

❸ To prepare the noodles, follow the instructions on the package (this varies by brand). Set aside.

❹ To assemble the sundaes, spoon about 1 tablespoon of the rose syrup mixture into the bottom of each of 4 sundae glasses. Divide the basil seeds and noodles evenly among the glasses, pressing down on them to ensure they are soaked in the syrup. Add a scoop of ice cream to each glass, then drizzle more syrup on the ice cream. Sprinkle each sundae with pomegranate seeds and serve right away with long spoons. When eating this sundae, be sure you dig to the bottom to get noodles and seeds in each bite.

POOJA'S TIP

Rose syrup is a concentrate used in beverage making. Rooh Afza is the best-known brand, but other brands can be used. Falooda sev are thin, dry vermicelli that become silky smooth when rehydrated. Tiny, black sweet basil seeds, known as sabja or tukmaria in Hindi, are commonly added to drinks in India. All of these can be found in Indian grocery stores and online, as can pomegranate molasses.

Malai Fruit Salad

Indian fruit salad, which combines several types of cut fresh fruit in sweetened milk, is a traditional dessert I grew up eating. It's like cold, sweet fruit soup, and although it is delicious, it was never decadent enough for me to call it "dessert." To make it more Malai friendly, I replaced the milk with ice cream and then added a star anise–spiced simple syrup to the fruit. But the best part? I top it all off with a mango-flavored cream cheese frosting. If you want to have a fruit salad for dessert, this is the way to do it. Choose the fruits you like for the salad. My favorites are strawberries, mangoes, pineapple, and blackberries.

MAKES 4 SERVINGS

FOR THE STAR ANISE SIMPLE SYRUP

½ cup granulated cane sugar

½ cup water

3 whole star anise

FOR THE MANGO CREAM CHEESE FROSTING

4 ounces cream cheese, at room temperature

3 tablespoons confectioners' sugar

¼ teaspoon salt

2–4 tablespoons mango purée (store-bought or homemade by blending fresh mango)

2 cups cut-up fresh fruit of choice (see headnote)

4 scoops Mango & Cream Ice Cream (page 42)

❶ To make the simple syrup, in a small saucepan, combine the granulated sugar, water, and star anise and bring to a boil over medium heat, stirring to dissolve the sugar, about 2 minutes. As soon as the mixture comes to a boil, remove from the heat and let cool to room temperature without discarding the star anise. Set aside.

❷ To make the frosting, in a bowl, using a wooden spoon, vigorously stir together the cream cheese, confectioners' sugar, and salt. When well mixed, add 2 tablespoons of the mango purée and mix well. Taste and add more mango to suit your palate.

❸ To assemble the salad, put the fruit into a bowl and drizzle about ¼ cup of the simple syrup over the top. Toss gently to make sure all the fruit pieces are coated with the syrup, then taste and add more syrup if needed. (Leftover syrup can be refrigerated in an airtight container for up to 2 weeks. Use it for drinks—or more fruit salad!)

❹ Transfer the fruit to a serving bowl. Arrange scoops of the ice cream over the fruit. Top the ice cream with dollops of the frosting. Enjoy immediately.

Ras Malai Frozen Tres Leches Cake

I love all things milk, so it's no surprise that tres leches cake is one of my favorite desserts. Why have one milk in your dessert when you can have three? The texture of the soaked cake always reminded me of the poached paneer that you find in traditional ras malai. Then one day I realized they have basically the same texture and composition: a soft, cake-like consistency in a pool of sweetened milk. So why have one dessert when you can have two in one? Ras Malai Frozen Tres Leches Cake is all of those things.

MAKES 20 SERVINGS

FOR THE CAKE

4 tablespoons unsalted butter, melted and cooled, plus room-temperature butter for the pan

½ cup neutral oil, such as grapeseed

¾ cup buttermilk

⅓ cup plain whole-milk yogurt

1 cup granulated cane sugar

1 teaspoon pure vanilla extract

1 tablespoon hot water

1½ cups all-purpose flour

1½ teaspoons baking powder

¾ teaspoon baking soda

¼ teaspoon salt

1 teaspoon ground cardamom

FOR THE CAKE SOAK

1 cup whole milk

⅔ cup sweetened condensed milk

1 cup evaporated milk

2 tablespoons rose water

1½ quarts Ras Malai Ice Cream (page 77), at room temperature for 5–7 minutes

❶ To make the cake, preheat the oven to 350°F. Butter the bottom and sides of a 9 x 13-inch baking pan.

❷ In a medium bowl, whisk together the butter, oil, buttermilk, yogurt, sugar, vanilla, and hot water, mixing well. In a large bowl, whisk together the flour, baking powder, baking soda, salt, and cardamom. Pour the butter mixture into the flour mixture and, using a rubber spatula, fold together until evenly mixed and the batter is smooth.

❸ Pour the batter into the prepared pan. Bake the cake until a toothpick inserted into the center comes out clean, about 30 minutes.

❹ While the cake bakes, make the cake soak. In a medium bowl, whisk together the whole milk, condensed milk, evaporated milk, and rose water, mixing well. Set aside.

❺ When the cake is ready, let cool in the pan on a wire rack for about 5 minutes. Then, using a toothpick, poke holes all over the top surface. Pour the cake soak evenly over the top and let the cake cool completely. As it cools, it will absorb the soak.

❻ Using an offset spatula, spread ice cream evenly on top, cut into pieces, and serve immediately.

Malpua with Fenugreek Ice Cream

When I first had malpua at a popular Indian restaurant, I was sold. It was a crisp, lightly fennel-scented pancake that was deep-fried and soaked in a sugar syrup and then served topped with a thick, creamy sweetened milk. It was decadent and delicious! I was in heaven. When picking it apart, I really did think of the fried part as a pancake, which made me wonder how it would taste with maple syrup. If you have made the fenugreek ice cream in this book, you already know that fenugreek takes on a maple-like flavor when heated with milk, so pairing a "pancake" with fenugreek ice cream felt natural. Make it, eat it, indulge.

**MAKES 16 PANCAKES;
4 SERVINGS**

1 cup all-purpose flour

1½ teaspoons fennel seeds, finely crushed in a spice grinder

¼ teaspoon ground cardamom

3 tablespoons nonfat milk powder

3 tablespoons plain whole-milk yogurt

1 cup water

½ cup granulated cane sugar

4 tablespoons ghee

½ teaspoon baking soda

1½ quarts Fenugreek Ice Cream with Walnuts (page 50)

1 In a bowl, whisk together the flour, crushed fennel seeds, and cardamom, mixing well. Whisk in the milk powder and yogurt until the mixture is evenly moistened. Add ½ cup of the water and stir with a wooden spoon until the mixture is thick and free flowing, similar to a pancake batter. Set aside for 30 minutes.

2 Meanwhile, in a small wide-rimmed saucepan, combine the sugar and the remaining ½ cup water over medium heat and bring to a simmer. Once the sugar has dissolved, continue to simmer, stirring occasionally, until the syrup registers 220°F on a candy thermometer (known as 1 string consistency in Indian cooking). Then reduce the heat to low to keep the syrup hot.

3 Line a large plate with paper towels and set it near the stove. Place a large frying pan over medium heat, add the ghee, and let it melt. While the ghee is heating, add the baking soda to the batter and stir to mix well. When the ghee is hot, ladle about ¼ cup of the batter into the pan for each pancake, being careful not to crowd them. (Each pancake will be 3–4 inches in diameter.) Fry until the underside is golden brown, about 2 minutes. Flip and fry until the second side is golden brown, about 3 minutes.

4 Using a spatula, transfer the pancakes to the towel-lined plate to drain briefly, then immediately place them in the sugar syrup. Using tongs, flip the pancakes in the syrup until well coated, then transfer to individual serving plates. Top each serving with a scoop of ice cream and serve right away. Repeat with the remaining batter.

Date & Nut Shake

In a very limited part of my life—the part when I played high school sports—my mom would make this shake for me as an energy booster. It was filled with nuts and protein and iron—all the good stuff—and, honestly, it was delicious. I felt like I was drinking a milkshake, even though she didn't use any ice cream. But you know me, always adding ice cream to things that don't call for it. This shake is super satisfying—nutty, creamy, spiced—and is the perfect after-school (or after-work) treat.

MAKES 2 SHAKES

¼ cup almonds

¼ cup walnuts

¼ cup pecans

6 Medjool dates, pitted

1 cup boiling water

½ teaspoon salt

¼ teaspoon ground cinnamon

Pinch of ground cardamom

1 cup whole milk

1 scoop ice cream, any flavor

❶ In a heatproof bowl, combine the almonds, walnuts, pecans, and dates and pour in the boiling water to cover. Let sit for 10 minutes and then drain.

❷ In a high-speed blender, combine the soaked nuts and dates, salt, cinnamon, cardamom, and milk and blend until smooth and creamy, about 2 minutes. Add the ice cream and pulse until well mixed and the mixture is the consistency of a milkshake. Pour into glasses and enjoy immediately.

POOJA'S TIP

I use any nuts I have on hand—often almonds, pecans, and walnuts, but sometimes hazelnuts, cashews, and pistachios. Even peanuts have made an appearance. Feel free to use your favorites. Using raw nuts will work well, but using roasted nuts gives a deeper, nuttier flavor.

Double Mango Cake

Can you tell that I love mango? This dessert combines a dense mango cake that seems almost custardy with a super creamy topping of Mango & Cream Ice Cream. It packs a real mango punch and is the ideal double-dessert combination. You can make this fancy by layering the ice cream and cake in a springform pan to get perfect ice cream cake slices, but I find it just as satisfying to scoop the ice cream on top of a slice.

MAKES 8–10 SERVINGS

2 cups all-purpose flour

2 teaspoons baking powder

½ teaspoon baking soda

½ cup neutral oil, such as grapeseed

1 cup granulated cane sugar

1½ cups sweetened mango pulp or mango purée (see Pooja's Tip)

¼ cup plain whole-milk yogurt

1½ quarts Mango & Cream Ice Cream (page 42)

1 Preheat the oven to 350°F. Line the bottom and sides of an 8-inch square baking pan with parchment paper.

In a bowl, whisk together the flour, baking powder, and baking soda. In a separate bowl, whisk together the oil, sugar, mango purée, and yogurt. Pour the mango mixture into the flour mixture and whisk to mix well.

2 Pour the batter into the prepared pan. Bake the cake until a toothpick inserted into the center comes out clean, about 40 minutes. Let cool completely in the pan on a wire rack. Invert the cake onto the rack, lift off the pan, and peel off the parchment.

3 Cut the cake into pieces and serve, topped with the ice cream.

POOJA'S TIP

For this recipe, it's best to use aam ras, or sweetened mango pulp, which can be found in cans at Indian grocery stores and online. The mango flavor is more concentrated and consistently sweet than in a purée, and it will make the flavor of the cake really pop!

Frozen Icebox Cake

I made my first icebox cake in college. It was a mix of graham crackers, store-bought vanilla pudding, and store-bought chocolate frosting. I would be grossly under exaggerating if I were to say that I was proud of that cake. I was wildly impressed with myself when I put it together, and it became my go-to dessert for a very long time. Thankfully, I have upped my icebox cake game since then, and now, of course, it includes ice cream. Orange Fennel and Coffee Cardamom have long been my favorite combination of Malai's ice cream flavors. Pair that with the dark chocolate of an Oreo cookie, and you have a dessert that's hard to beat.

MAKES 10 SERVINGS

1 package (10.1 ounces) Oreo Thins

1 pint Orange Fennel Ice Cream (page 45), at room temperature for about 20 minutes

1 pint Coffee Cardamom Ice Cream (page 37), at room temperature for about 20 minutes

1 cup heavy cream

2 tablespoons granulated cane sugar

1. Line the bottom and sides of an 8-inch square baking dish with parchment paper. Lay one-third of the cookies in a single layer on the bottom of the prepared dish, making sure to cover it completely and breaking the cookies as needed to make them fit. Scoop the Orange Fennel Ice Cream on top of the cookies and, using an offset or rubber spatula, smooth it out in an even layer, covering the cookies completely.

2. Top the ice cream with another layer of cookies. Scoop the Coffee Cardamom Ice Cream on top of the second layer of cookies and smooth it out in an even layer. Top with a final layer of cookies, covering the ice cream completely. Place the baking dish in the freezer while you make the whipped cream.

3. In a bowl, using an electric mixer, beat together the cream and sugar on medium speed until soft peaks form, 3–4 minutes.

4. Remove the baking dish from the freezer and top the final cookie layer with the whipped cream, spreading it evenly. Lightly cover the dish with plastic wrap and place it in the freezer overnight before serving.

5. When ready to serve, remove from the freezer, slice, and serve.

Frozen Chocolate Biscuit Cake

I'm not shy about my love of chai, and my love of biscuits is nearly as strong. After all, what's a cup of tea without something to dip into it? Tea biscuits, specifically digestives, can always be found in my pantry (or more likely, right on my kitchen table). But they take on a whole new form in this rich and satisfying biscuit cake. They're mixed right into ice cream and melted chocolate and take on a crunchy yet soft texture. This dessert is a breeze to put together, and you can snack on leftovers directly from the freezer.

MAKES 10 SERVINGS

½ cup unsalted butter, cut into pieces, plus more for the baking dish

1 package (14 ounces) digestive biscuits, rich tea biscuits, or graham crackers, crumbled into 1-inch pieces

½ cup chopped hazelnuts or nuts of choice

½ cup dried cherries or dried fruit of choice, cut to size of cherries

5 ounces dark chocolate, coarsely chopped

5 ounces milk chocolate, coarsely chopped

¼ teaspoon salt

1 pint Sweet Milk Ice Cream (page 31) or flavor of choice, at room temperature for 5–7 minutes

1 cup dark chocolate chips

1. Butter the bottom and sides of an 8-inch square baking dish, a 9-inch round springform pan, or any dish or pan of similar size. Line the bottom and sides with parchment paper and then butter the parchment.

2. In a large bowl, stir together the biscuits. nuts, and cherries. Set aside.

3. In the top of a double boiler, combine the butter, chopped dark chocolate, milk chocolate, and salt. Place over (not touching) simmering water in the lower pan and heat, stirring occasionally, just until the butter and chocolate have melted and the mixture is smooth and thick. Remove from the heat and let cool completely.

4. Add the ice cream to the cooled chocolate mixture and stir until well mixed. Pour the chocolate–ice cream mixture over the biscuit mixture and stir until the biscuit mixture is evenly coated. Pour into the prepared dish and pat down the surface to ensure the cake will take the shape of the dish. Cover and place in the freezer for 2 hours.

5. About 10 minutes before the cake is ready to come out of the freezer, put the chocolate chips into a microwave-safe bowl and microwave in 30-second bursts, stirring after each burst, until the chips are melted. Let cool for about 3 minutes.

6. Remove the cake from the freezer, invert it onto a serving plate, lift off the dish or pan, and peel off the parchment. (If using a springform pan, unclasp and lift off the sides, then invert onto the plate, lift off the base, and peel off the parchment.) Turn the cake right side up and pour the melted chocolate in the center of the cake. Using an offset spatula, spread the chocolate so it covers the top and runs down the sides. Return the cake to the freezer for about 15 minutes to set the chocolate, then remove from the freezer, slice, and serve.

Spiced Peanut Butter Froyo Pie

There is no one that loves a peanut butter pie more than my sister. There is no one that loves a quick and simple dessert recipe more than my sister. Both of these things are found in the overlapping Venn diagram that is this recipe. It's quick and easy and has all of the satisfying flavors of peanut butter pie (with the unexpected addition of star anise). If you have Peanut Chikki and chocolate chips on hand, they are great add-ins, but this pie is just as tasty without them.

MAKES 8–10 SERVINGS

2 cups vanilla whole-milk yogurt

1¼ cups creamy natural peanut butter

1 cup whole milk

¼ cup agave nectar or honey

¾ teaspoon ground star anise (see Pooja's Tip, page 88)

½ cup Peanut Chikki (page 196) (optional)

½ cup mini chocolate chips, plus more for sprinkling (optional)

One 9-inch store-bought no-bake chocolate pie crust

❶ In a blender, combine the yogurt, peanut butter, milk, agave nectar, and star anise and blend until completely smooth, about 2 minutes. Transfer to an airtight container and refrigerate to chill and firm up, about 2 hours.

❷ Remove from the refrigerator, add the Peanut Chikki and chocolate chips, if using, and stir to mix well. Pour the mixture into the pie crust and sprinkle the top with chocolate chips, if using. Cover and place in the freezer until firm, about 2 hours.

❸ Remove from the freezer, slice, and serve.

Parle-G Masala Chai
Ice Cream Sandwiches

For Indian Americans, there is nothing more iconic than a crisp Parle-G biscuit being dunked into a steaming-hot cup of masala chai. It's the quintessential pairing, so it was easy to translate into an ice cream sandwich with our Masala Chai Ice Cream! Eat them as soon as you make them and you get the crunchy bite. Leave them in the freezer, and the cookies become super soft and taste almost like they have been dunked into chai. Both are equally delicious and nostalgic.

MAKES 18 SANDWICHES

1 package (11.9 ounces) Parle-G biscuits

2 tablespoons coconut oil

½ teaspoon salt

1–2 tablespoons heavy cream, or more if needed

1 quart Masala Chai Ice Cream (page 38), at room temperature for 3–5 minutes

MALAI FUN FACT

We bring these ice cream sandwiches back every year for Diwali, and we can never keep them in stock. They're the most requested, most popular item we have during the holiday.

① To make the cookie butter, add 3 sleeves of the biscuits from the Parle-G package to a food processor and process until reduced to fine crumbs. Add the coconut oil, salt, and 1 tablespoon of the cream and process until well blended and a butter consistency forms, about 2 minutes. Add more cream if needed to achieve the desired consistency. It should be spreadable, like a nut butter.

② Line the bottom and sides of a quarter sheet pan (9 x 13 inches) with parchment paper. Scoop out the ice cream onto the prepared pan and, using a rubber spatula, spread it to the edges of the pan in an even layer. Place in the freezer until frozen solid, about 1 hour.

③ Lay half of the remaining biscuits, bottom side up, on a sheet pan. Spread about 1 teaspoon of the cookie butter on each of the biscuits. Place the sheet pan in the freezer.

④ Remove the sheet pan with the ice cream from the freezer. Using a biscuit as a template, score the ice cream to the size of the biscuits. If the ice cream becomes too soft, stick the sheet pan back into the freezer until the ice cream firms up.

⑤ When the entire sheet of ice cream has been scored, remove the sheet pan with the butter-topped biscuits from the freezer. Using a spatula, place a piece of ice cream directly on each butter-topped biscuit, then top with the remaining biscuits, bottom side down. Place the prepared sandwiches back in the freezer until they are completely frozen before serving. To store leftovers, place in an airtight container and freeze for up to 1 month.

Lemon Cardamom Frozen Cheesecake

Growing up, cardamom was often in Indian sweets I would eat, but only as big seeds. I would be eating a delicious dessert when I would bite into a seed, and all the spice would explode in my mouth. As a six-year-old, I wasn't impressed. As a result, my mom would make all her sweets without cardamom. So I wasn't a cardamom fan—until Malai. When used well, it's the perfect complement to many flavors, including lemon, which is its partner in this light, refreshing, creamy cheesecake.

MAKES 10 SERVINGS

FOR THE CRUST

1½ cups graham cracker crumbs (from about 12 crackers) (see Pooja's Tip)

¼ cup granulated cane sugar

½ cup unsalted butter, melted

¼ teaspoon salt

FOR THE CHEESECAKE FILLING

1 package (8 ounces) cream cheese, at room temperature

¾ cup sweetened condensed milk

½ cup heavy cream

¼ cup Sweet Milk Ice Cream (page 31)

2 teaspoons grated lemon zest

2 teaspoons fresh lemon juice

½ teaspoon ground cardamom

FOR THE STRAWBERRY TOPPING

½ cup granulated cane sugar

⅓ cup honey

¼ cup water

2 tablespoons fresh lemon juice

¼ cup Sweet Milk Ice Cream

2 cups strawberries, hulled and cut into small pieces

❶ Line the bottom and sides of a 9-inch pie pan or 8-inch square baking dish with parchment paper, allowing the sides to extend above the rim by 1–2 inches.

❷ To make the crust, in a bowl, stir together the graham cracker crumbs, sugar, butter, and salt until well mixed and evenly moistened. Pour the crust mixture into the center of the prepared pan and, using your fingers, press it evenly onto the bottom and about 1 inch up the sides of the pan. Place the crust in the freezer while you prepare the filling.

❸ To make the filling, in a large bowl, using an electric mixer, beat together the cream cheese, condensed milk, cream, ice cream, lemon zest and juice, and cardamom on medium speed until well mixed and smooth, about 2 minutes.

❹ Remove the crust from the freezer and pour in the filling. Return to the freezer and freeze until the filling is solid, 2–3 hours.

❺ Meanwhile, make the topping. In a saucepan, combine the sugar, honey, water, lemon juice, ice cream, and strawberries over medium heat and cook, stirring often, until the sugar dissolves and you feel no grittiness as you stir, 4–5 minutes. Remove from the heat and let cool completely.

❻ Pour the cooled topping over the frozen cheesecake, then freeze the fully assembled dessert for an additional 2 hours. To serve, using the parchment, lift the cheesecake out of the pan. Peel away the parchment, set the cheesecake on a serving plate, cut into slices, and serve.

POOJA'S TIP

To make the graham cracker crumbs, put the crackers into a food processor and process until reduced to fine crumbs. Alternatively, put the crackers in a ziplock bag and crush with a rolling pin.

Fried Ice Cream Pie

When my family lived in Pennsylvania, there was a Mexican restaurant nearby, Chi Chi's, which was our go-to for birthdays and other celebrations. The food was delicious, but the desserts were spectacular. Among them was fried ice cream. It was a rich vanilla ice cream, battered and deep-fried until it had a crisp, crackly topping, then drizzled with honey and chocolate sauce and served with whipped cream and a cherry on top. This is that same dessert in pie form, and suitable to serve a crowd—because there is never enough fried ice cream in our lives. Don't skip the honey!

MAKES 10 SERVINGS

Nonstick cooking spray, for the pan

½ cup unsalted butter, cubed

2 cups crushed cornflakes (measure after crushing in a Ziplock bag)

3 tablespoons granulated cane sugar

3 teaspoons ground cinnamon

¾ teaspoon salt

1¾ cups heavy cream

¼ cup evaporated milk

1 can (14 ounces) sweetened condensed milk

1 teaspoon pure vanilla extract

1½–2 cups Spiced Whipped Cream, made with cinnamon (page 204)

Spiced Honey (page 195), for drizzling

1 Spray the bottom and sides of an 8-inch square baking pan or a 9-inch round springform pan with cooking spray.

2 In a saucepan, melt the butter over medium heat until it is liquid. Then, using a wooden spoon, begin stirring constantly. The butter will begin foaming on top and then the foam will subside and brown bits will start to form on the bottom of the pan. Add the cornflakes, sugar, 1½ teaspoons of the cinnamon, and ¼ teaspoon of the salt and stir to ensure all the ingredients are evenly distributed and well mixed. Continue stirring over medium heat until the cornflakes are toasted, about 5 minutes. Remove from the heat and let cool completely.

3 Meanwhile, make the ice cream. In a large bowl, using an electric mixer, beat together the cream and evaporated milk on medium speed until soft peaks form, about 5 minutes. Add the condensed milk, vanilla, and the remaining 1½ teaspoons cinnamon and ½ teaspoon salt and continue to beat on high speed until well mixed, creamy, and stiff, another 1–2 minutes.

4 Layer half of the cooled cornflakes mixture in the prepared pan, pressing down to form a compact layer. Pour the ice cream mixture evenly over the top, then top with the remaining cornflakes mixture and lightly press down with an offset spatula. Cover and place in the freezer until set, about 4 hours.

5 To serve, remove from the freezer. If using a square baking pan, serve the pie directly from the pan. If using a springform pan, unclasp and lift off the sides, then slide the pie onto a serving plate. Top the pie with the whipped cream and drizzle on the honey.

Easiest Ice Cream Sandwiches

The day I learned that basic white sandwich bread could be used as a crust for desserts, my life changed. Suddenly, I did not have to plan ahead to make a pie or a tart. Rolled out and baked, white sandwich bread can be the perfect liner for stewed berries, custard, and, yes, ice cream. Here, instead of using the bread as a pie crust, I fry up slices to make ice cream sandwiches—a true dessert sandwich.

MAKES 3 SANDWICHES

6 slices white sandwich bread, such as Wonder Bread

3 teaspoons ghee

1 tablespoon granulated cane sugar

½ teaspoon salt

¼ teaspoon ground cardamom

1 pint ice cream, any flavor

❶ Cut the crusts off all the bread slices. Using a rolling pin, roll out each slice until it's flattened and as thin as possible.

❷ Using a 2–3-inch round cookie cutter or an overturned water glass, trace and cut out a circle from each bread slice.

❸ In a small nonstick frying pan, heat 1½ teaspoons of the ghee over medium-high heat. While the ghee is heating, in a shallow bowl, stir together the sugar, salt, and cardamom.

❹ When the ghee is hot, place 3 bread circles in the pan and fry until golden brown on the underside, 1–1½ minutes. Flip the bread circles and fry on the second side until golden brown, 1–1½ minutes.

❺ Using a spatula, immediately transfer the bread circles to the sweet-salty cardamom mixture, coating the circles on both sides, and transfer to a large plate. Add the remaining 1½ teaspoons ghee to the pan and fry and then coat the remaining bread circles the same way.

❻ Top 3 fried bread circles with a scoop of ice cream. Place another fried bread circle on top of each scoop and enjoy right away.

Mini Strawberry Ice Cream Pies

Given my sweet tooth, it is not surprising that my first memory of a strawberry is of one in a pie. It was a strawberry cream pie that my family would pick up from a department store sweets section whenever we had company. The tastiest, freshest whole strawberries were swirled with a jam, tucked into a buttery graham cracker crust, and topped with mounds and mounds of cloud-like whipped cream. I still dream of that pie. The frozen version does not involve any jam making, but you still get syrupy berries and a crunchy crust topped with cold, creamy ice cream—the best of summer in a bite.

MAKES 24 MINI PIES

FOR THE FILLING

4 cups strawberries, finely diced

2½ tablespoons granulated cane sugar

Juice from ½ lemon

½ teaspoon ground fennel (see Pooja's Tip, page 168)

FOR THE CRUST

Nonstick cooking spray, for the muffin cups

9 graham cracker sheets (18 squares)

4 teaspoons granulated cane sugar

Pinch of salt

6 tablespoons unsalted butter, melted

1 pint ice cream, any flavor

❶ In a bowl, combine the strawberries, sugar, lemon juice, and fennel and stir to mix well. Cover and refrigerate for 2 hours. Meanwhile, make the crust.

❷ Preheat the oven to 350°F. Spray 24 mini muffin cups with cooking spray.

❸ In a food processor, process the graham crackers until reduced to fine crumbs. (Alternatively, place them in a large ziplock bag and crush with a rolling pin.) Transfer to a bowl, add the sugar, salt, and butter, and stir until well mixed and evenly moistened.

❹ Spoon 1 tablespoon of the crust mixture into each prepared muffin cup. Set aside the remaining crust mixture. Using the back of the tablespoon measure, press the crumbs evenly onto the bottom and up the sides of each cup. Bake the crusts until golden brown, 7–8 minutes. Let cool completely in the pan on a wire rack.

❺ Remove the filling from the refrigerator and drain into a fine-mesh sieve set over a bowl. Add the drained filling to the reserved crust mixture and mix well. Reserve the liquid. Fill each crust with a spoonful of filling. Top each pie with a spoonful of ice cream and a drizzle of the reserved liquid and enjoy immediately.

Ice Cream Peda

When I was growing up, our family had a monthly tradition of all piling into the car and driving to the nearest Indian grocery store. My favorite part of the trip was the sweets case. Without fail, we would treat ourselves to a box of peda, a milk fudge that was faintly spiced with saffron and topped with pistachios. Making peda is not easy, as you need to boil down milk until all the water has evaporated and you are left with only the milk solids. But with a little help from ice cream and milk powder, here is a shortcut version that is just as delicious.

MAKES 24 PIECES

1 teaspoon packed saffron threads

¼ cup boiling water

1 quart Sweet Milk Ice Cream (page 31)

¼ teaspoon salt

4 cups whole-milk powder

Ghee, for greasing your hands

About ½ cup chopped pistachios or 24 whole almonds

❶ To bloom the saffron, crush the saffron threads with your fingers and drop them into a small heatproof bowl. Add the boiling water and let sit to develop the flavor, at least 5 minutes or up to 20 minutes.

❷ Scoop the ice cream into a large nonstick frying pan. Place the pan over medium heat and let the ice cream melt. As it melts, add the bloomed saffron and salt. Once melted, add the milk powder and, using a rubber spatula or a wooden spoon, stir until well incorporated. Reduce the heat to medium low and cook, stirring constantly to prevent scorching, until the mixture starts to pull away from the sides of the pan, about 15 minutes.

❸ Remove from the heat and let the mixture cool until it can be handled, about 5 minutes. Meanwhile, line a sheet pan with parchment paper. When the mixture is cool enough to handle, turn it out onto a work surface, coat your hands with ghee, and knead until smooth, about 5 minutes.

❹ To shape each sweet, coat your hands with ghee, then pinch off a golf-ball-size piece of the mixture and roll between your palms into a smooth ball. Flatten the ball slightly, press down on the center with your thumb to create an indentation, and then place on the prepared sheet pan. Repeat until all the mixture has been shaped, adding more ghee to your hands as needed. You should have 24 shaped pieces.

❺ Set a few chopped pistachios or 1 whole almond in each indentation and press down lightly to ensure the nuts stick. Refrigerate until cold, about 2 hours. Serve chilled.

Chocolate Chili Ice Cream Bars

This is the very last recipe I wrote for this book (I didn't write them in order), and it was only when I had just one more recipe to do that I realized I did not have a proper chocolate chocolate chocolate dessert! I know why that's the case: that kind of dessert just doesn't appeal to me, and I always need something to cut the richness of the chocolate. But who am I to decide what you like? You should have the most chocolaty option, and this is it! It is delicious, and trust me, it even made me into a chocolate convert.

MAKES 10 BARS

FOR THE CRUST

2 cups chocolate cookie or chocolate wafer crumbs (from about 22 cookies)

½ cup unsalted butter, melted

½ teaspoon salt

FOR THE CHOCOLATE CHILI ICE CREAM

1 can (14 ounces) sweetened condensed milk

½ cup unsweetened natural cocoa powder

1 teaspoon pure vanilla extract

1½ teaspoons cayenne pepper

¼ teaspoon salt

2 cups heavy cream

Magic Shell with cardamom omitted (page 200)

1 Line the bottom and sides of an 8-inch square baking dish with parchment paper, allowing the sides to extend above the rim by 1–2 inches.

2 To make the crust, in a food processor, process the chocolate cookies or wafers until reduced to fine crumbs. (Alternatively, place them in a large ziplock bag and crush with a rolling pin.) Transfer to a medium bowl, and combine with the butter and salt. Stir until well mixed and evenly moistened. Pour the mixture into the prepared pan and, using your fingers, press it evenly over the bottom. Place the crust in the freezer while you prepare the ice cream.

3 To make the ice cream, in a medium bowl, whisk together the condensed milk, cocoa powder, vanilla, cayenne, and salt, mixing well.

4 In a large bowl, using an electric mixer, beat the cream on medium-high speed until stiff peaks form, about 5 minutes. Using a rubber spatula, fold 1 cup of the whipped cream into the condensed milk mixture just until combined. Then fold the condensed milk mixture into the rest of the whipped cream until evenly combined.

5 Remove the crust from the freezer and pour in the ice cream mixture. Return the dish to the freezer and freeze for at least 4 hours or preferably overnight.

6 About 5 minutes before serving, remove the dish from the freezer. Pour the Magic Shell on top of the frozen ice cream and let set before serving. Cut into bars to serve.

Pooja's Perfect Malai Ice Cream Sundae

I know that sundaes don't need a recipe. But I'm putting one here just in case you need inspiration. You may think this is too much—too much ice cream, too many sauces, too much *stuff*. But trust me when I say that it's perfect. It all works so well together—the order of layering is important here—and the end result is nothing short of magic.

**SERVES 1 HUNGRY
ICE CREAM LOVER**

1 slice **Coffee Orange
Tea Cake** (page 172)

**Jaggery Fennel Caramel
Sauce** (page 191), for drizzling

1 scoop **Coffee Cardamom
Ice Cream** (page 37)

1 scoop **Orange Fennel
Ice Cream** (page 45)

Chocolate Cardamom Sauce
(page 186), for drizzling

Spiced Whipped Cream
(page 204), for dolloping

Cone Crunch (page 192),
for sprinkling

Cherry Rose Syrup (page 189),
for drizzling

❶ Place the cake on the bottom of a cake plate or a wide, shallow bowl. Generously drizzle the Jaggery Fennel Caramel Sauce over the cake. Place both scoops of ice cream on top of the caramel sauce. Generously drizzle Chocolate Cardamom Sauce over the ice cream. Dollop the whipped cream on top of the ice cream. Sprinkle the Cone Crunch on top of the whipped cream. Lightly drizzle the Cherry Rose Syrup on top of the whipped cream and Cone Crunch. Serve immediately.

Baked Goods

Orange Cardamom Mini Muffins

I was on Food Network's *Chopped Sweets* a few years ago, and I won! And I believe it was these orange cardamom muffins that sealed my win. They are fluffy and bouncy, bright and delicious. They soak up any ice cream you serve them with but are also the perfect texture when frozen: cut them in half, stick a mini scoop of ice cream between the halves, and freeze. They're bite size and the ideal treat when you are looking for something a little sweet. What can I say? They're winners!

MAKES 24 MINI MUFFINS

Nonstick cooking spray, for the muffin cups

1 cup granulated cane sugar

Grated zest of 1 orange

¾ cup buttermilk

4 tablespoons unsalted butter, melted and cooled

¼ cup neutral oil, such as canola or grapeseed

¼ cup plain whole-milk yogurt

1 tablespoon ground cardamom

1 teaspoon pure vanilla extract

1¾ cups all-purpose flour

1½ teaspoons baking powder

½ teaspoon baking soda

½ teaspoon salt

❶ Preheat the oven to 350°F. Spray 24 mini muffin cups with cooking spray.

❷ In a large bowl, stir together the sugar and orange zest. Using your fingers, rub the orange zest into the sugar, coating the sugar well and releasing the essential oils in the zest. Add the buttermilk, butter, oil, yogurt, cardamom, and vanilla and stir to mix well.

❸ In a medium bowl, whisk together the flour, baking powder, baking soda, and salt. Fold the flour mixture into the buttermilk mixture just until thoroughly incorporated. Spoon the batter into the prepared muffins cups, filling each cup to the rim.

❹ Bake the muffins until they spring back when lightly touched, about 10 minutes. Turn out onto a wire rack and let cool completely.

Almond Butter & Cardamom Cookies

Sometimes you need a baked good that's super easy to put together and seemingly simple in taste just to deceive everyone—even yourself. These cookies are that. The ingredient list is short and unassuming, and the cookies are not much to look at when they emerge from the oven. But these gems are what I crave when I want something to nibble on. They are great on their own, soft enough to freeze for an ice cream sandwich, and delicious as an ice cream mix-in. Don't sleep on these sleeper hits.

MAKES 24 COOKIES

1 cup all-purpose flour

½ teaspoon baking soda

½ teaspoon salt

½ cup agave nectar, honey, or grade A maple syrup

½ cup natural almond butter

3 tablespoons unsalted butter, melted and cooled

½ teaspoon pure vanilla extract

½ teaspoon ground cardamom

Flaky sea salt, for sprinkling

1 Position a rack in the top third of the oven and preheat the oven to 350°F. Line a sheet pan with parchment paper.

2 In a medium bowl, whisk together the flour, baking soda, and salt. In a small bowl, whisk together the agave nectar, almond butter, butter, vanilla, and cardamom, mixing well. Pour the agave nectar mixture into the flour mixture and fold together just until thoroughly incorporated.

3 Spoon tablespoonfuls of the batter onto the prepared sheet pan, spacing them about 2 inches apart. Sprinkle with sea salt. Bake the cookies until they start to take on some color, about 10 minutes. Let cool on the pan on a wire rack for 5 minutes, then transfer to the rack and let cool completely.

Ba's Favorite Vanilla Cake

Ba, my maternal grandmother, was one of my most favorite people in the world and the inspiration behind so many of these recipes. She was wildly talented in the kitchen, whipping out recipes like no one else. I'm still craving to recreate some of them, but I get nowhere close. I don't have her touch, her skilled hand. But when it came to cake, her approach was fairly simple. She always wanted an unadorned, uncomplicated vanilla cake, forks optional. I asked my aunt for the recipe, and this is the exact cake that my grandmother made year after year. Ba may have liked it simple, but I added a lovely saffron glaze that I think complements it perfectly.

MAKES 6–8 SERVINGS

FOR THE CAKE

Nonstick cooking spray, for the pan

1 cup self-rising flour

1 teaspoon baking powder

½ teaspoon baking soda

¾ cup sweetened condensed milk

5 tablespoons unsalted butter, melted and cooled

1 teaspoon pure vanilla extract

½ teaspoon salt

⅓ cup water

FOR THE GLAZE

¼ teaspoon packed saffron threads

1 tablespoon boiling water

2 cups confectioners' sugar

¼ cup heavy cream

Juice of 1 lemon

❶ Preheat the oven to 400°F. Spray the bottom and sides of a 6-inch round cake pan with cooking spray.

❷ To make the cake, in a medium bowl, sift together the flour, baking powder, and baking soda. In a large bowl, stir together the condensed milk, butter, vanilla, and salt, mixing well. Add the flour mixture to the condensed milk mixture and fold in with a rubber spatula until no dry ingredient streaks remain. Add the water and mix until the batter is cohesive.

❸ Pour the batter into the prepared pan. Bake the cake for 10 minutes. Reduce the oven temperature to 300°F and bake until the top of the cake is golden brown and springs back when lightly touched and a toothpick inserted into the center comes out clean, about 10 minutes longer. Let cool in the pan on a wire rack for about 10 minutes, then turn the cake out onto the rack, turn upright, and let cool completely.

❹ While the cake is cooling, make the glaze. To bloom the saffron, crush the saffron threads with your fingers and drop them into a small heatproof bowl. Add the boiling water and let sit to develop the flavor, at least 5 minutes or up to 20 minutes.

❺ Sift the confectioners' sugar into a medium bowl. Add the cream, lemon juice, and bloomed saffron and whisk together until smooth.

❻ Set the cooled cake on a serving plate. Pour the glaze over the center of the cake, letting it drip down the sides. Let the cake sit for about 5 minutes to allow the glaze to harden, then serve.

Malai's Perfect Chocolate Chip Cookies

I'm obviously biased, but I promise you that Malai makes the most perfect chocolate chip cookie. It's crispy on the edges, gooey in the middle, packed with three different kinds of chocolate, and, of course, has the unexpected spice. This time, that spice is star anise. There is just enough of it to make you love the cookie even more and wonder what's in it, but not enough to overwhelm or overpower the simplicity of a classic chocolate chip cookie. Because Malai uses very specific chocolates in our version, I've revamped the recipe for more readily available ingredients, but the end result is just as delicious.

MAKES 12 COOKIES

3 tablespoons unsalted butter, at room temperature

¼ teaspoon ground star anise (see Pooja's Tip, page 88)

½ cup packed dark brown sugar

2 tablespoons plain whole-milk yogurt

½ teaspoon pure vanilla extract

½ cup all-purpose flour

2 tablespoons cornstarch

¼ teaspoon baking powder

¼ teaspoon baking soda

¾ teaspoon salt

⅓ cup milk chocolate discs

¼ cup dark chocolate chips

¼ cup chopped white chocolate

1. Preheat the oven to 325°F. Line 2 sheet pans with parchment paper.

2. In a large bowl, using an electric mixer, beat together the butter, star anise, and brown sugar on medium speed until well blended and fluffy, 3–4 minutes. Add the yogurt and vanilla and beat until incorporated.

3. In a medium bowl, whisk together the flour, cornstarch, baking powder, baking soda, and salt. On medium speed, add the flour mixture to the butter mixture and beat just until blended, about 30 seconds. Using a rubber spatula, fold in the milk, dark, and white chocolates.

4. Using a roughly 2-tablespoon cookie scoop, scoop out balls of the dough onto the prepared sheet pans, spacing them about 1 inch apart.

5. Bake the cookies until crispy on the edges, about 15 minutes. Let cool on the pans on wire racks for 2 minutes, then transfer to the racks and let cool completely.

Cardamom Snickerdoodles

My first foray into having my own business was when I was working for a nonprofit right out of college. I made desserts during my nonwork hours and decided to turn my "hobby" into a little business called Sweets by Pooja. The quality of the desserts made up for the lack of originality in the business name. The most popular order by far was the snickerdoodles. In those days, I always wondered if they would be just as popular if I made them with cardamom instead of the traditional cinnamon. That question was answered when I started Malai and offered a cardamom snickerdoodle. Yes, they are, in fact, very, very popular. And these cookies make great ice cream sandwiches.

MAKES 12 COOKIES

¾ cup plus 1 tablespoon all-purpose flour

1 tablespoon baking powder

½ cup plus 2 tablespoons unsalted butter, at room temperature

1¾ cups granulated cane sugar

1 teaspoon salt

½ cup honey

3 tablespoons whole milk

1 tablespoon ground cardamom

❶ Preheat the oven to 325°F. Line 2 sheet pans with parchment paper.

❷ In a small bowl, whisk together the flour and baking powder. In a large bowl, using an electric mixer, beat together the butter, ¾ cup of the sugar, ½ teaspoon of the salt, the honey, and milk on medium speed until well blended and fluffy, 3–4 minutes. On medium speed, add the flour mixture and beat just until blended, about 1½ minutes.

❸ In a small, shallow bowl, stir together the remaining 1 cup sugar, the remaining ½ teaspoon salt, and the cardamom.

❹ Using a roughly 2-tablespoon cookie scoop, scoop out a ball of the dough and drop it into the bowl of cardamom sugar. Flatten the dough ball in the sugar mixture, coating it on both sides and flattening to about 2 inches in diameter. Transfer the cookie to a prepared sheet pan. Repeat with the remaining dough, spacing the cookies about 1 inch apart on the pans.

❺ Bake the cookies until lightly golden, about 12 minutes. Let cool on the pans on wire racks for 2 minutes, then transfer to the racks and let cool completely. To turn these into an ice cream sandwich, place a scoop of your favorite ice cream between two cooled cookies and enjoy immediately.

Butterscotch Fennel Loaf

Butterscotch is one of the most underrated flavors. It has the reputation of being overly sweet and sugary. But it's not! It's nuanced. It has natural cooked notes, sugar that is complex and burnt, and a deep caramel flavor. Butterscotch is quite wonderful on its own, but pair butterscotch with the woodsy, licorice notes of fennel and it becomes next level. We sometimes serve this loaf cake at Malai, and I can't wait to have a slice when it's on the menu. I'm on a mission to make this everyone's favorite!

MAKES 8–10 SERVINGS

Nonstick cooking spray, for the pan

2 cups all-purpose flour

1 teaspoon baking powder

½ teaspoon baking soda

1 teaspoon salt

2 tablespoons ground fennel (see Pooja's Tip)

1 cup unsalted butter

1¾ cups packed light brown sugar

¾ cup plain whole-milk yogurt

⅓ cup butterscotch chips

1. Preheat the oven to 350°F. Spray the bottom and sides of a 9 x 5-inch loaf pan with cooking spray.

2. In a medium bowl, whisk together the flour, baking powder, baking soda, salt, and fennel.

3. In a medium saucepan, melt the butter over medium heat. Once the butter is melted, remove the pan from the heat and whisk in the sugar and yogurt until the sugar dissolves and all the ingredients are well blended. Using a rubber spatula, fold in the flour mixture until no dry ingredient streaks remain. Then fold in the butterscotch chips, mixing evenly.

4. Transfer the batter to the prepared pan. Bake the loaf cake until the top is golden brown and a toothpick inserted into the center comes out clean, 30–40 minutes. Let cool completely in the pan on a wire rack before serving.

POOJA'S TIP

If you can't find ground fennel, toast 2 tablespoons fennel seeds in a dry frying pan over medium heat for about 5 minutes, stirring constantly, until just toasted. Remove from the heat, let cool, then grind in a spice grinder to a powder. Store any ground fennel you don't need for the recipe in an airtight container in the pantry.

Black Cardamom Graham Crackers

I love learning about new spices, and black cardamom is one of them. I've long known about the variety that is the floral, warming spice, but did not know that it was specifically green cardamom. Black cardamom, in contrast, is a bit funkier. It's smoky, has menthol notes, and is very woodsy. And this specific cardamom is nothing short of perfect in this hearty graham cracker.

MAKES 10–12 CRACKERS

1¼ cups whole-wheat flour

1¼ cups all-purpose flour, plus more for dusting

1½ teaspoons baking soda

½ teaspoon ground black cardamom

¼ teaspoon salt

¾ cup unsalted butter, at room temperature

¾ cup granulated cane sugar

¼ cup molasses

1 Preheat the oven to 350°F. Line a sheet pan with parchment paper.

2 In a medium bowl, whisk together the whole-wheat and all-purpose flours, baking soda, cardamom, and salt.

3 In a large bowl, using an electric mixer, beat together the butter, sugar, and molasses on medium speed until fluffy, 3–4 minutes. On low speed, slowly add the flour mixture and beat until fully incorporated and a smooth dough forms.

4 Dust a work surface and a rolling pin with flour. Transfer the dough to the floured surface and roll out into a rectangle about ¼ inch thick. Transfer the dough to the prepared sheet pan. With a fork, prick the dough all over to ensure that it doesn't puff up in the oven.

5 Bake until the top of the rectangle is darker and the edges are crisp, 10–12 minutes. Let cool completely on the pan on a wire rack, then, using your hands, break the sheet into crackers for serving.

Melted Ice Cream Cake

Does anyone remember when melted ice cream cake was all the rage on social media? When people would mix a pint of melted ice cream with self-rising flour and call it cake? Of course I had to try it. I added a little fat for moisture, more sugar, and even a glaze to pump up the flavor of the ice cream. Results? It's rich, satisfying, and amazingly easy. When I make this cake, I often use pints of ice cream that have developed an iciness after sitting in the freezer too long. That icy flavor melts away in the cake, so I know it will go unnoticed.

MAKES 8–10 SERVINGS

FOR THE CAKE

Nonstick cooking spray, for the pan

1½ cups all-purpose flour

2 teaspoons baking powder

½ teaspoon salt

¼ cup granulated cane sugar

2 tablespoons coconut oil, melted

1 pint ice cream, melted (best with Masala Chai, page 38)

FOR THE GLAZE

½ cup confectioners' sugar

2 tablespoons heavy cream

½ teaspoon ground spices, such as cinnamon or Malai Chai Masala (see Malai Fun Fact, page 38)

¼ teaspoon salt

❶ Preheat the oven to 350°F. Spray the bottom and sides of a 9 x 5-inch loaf pan with cooking spray.

❷ To make the cake, in a medium bowl, whisk together the flour, baking powder, and salt.

❸ In a large bowl, whisk together the granulated sugar and coconut oil until well mixed. Add the melted ice cream and stir until fully incorporated. Using a rubber spatula, fold in the flour mixture until no dry ingredient streaks remain.

❹ Pour the batter into the prepared pan. Bake the cake until a toothpick inserted into the center comes out clean, about 35 minutes. Let cool completely in the pan on a wire rack.

❺ While the cake is baking, make the glaze. Sift the confectioners' sugar into a medium bowl. Add the cream, spices, and salt and whisk until smooth.

❻ Once the cake has cooled, pour the glaze over the top. Let the cake sit for 15 minutes to allow the glaze to harden, then slice and serve.

Coffee Orange Tea Cake

One of my favorite restaurants in my parents' hometown in India serves various flavors of ice cream, both seasonal and year-round. One flavor that never leaves the menu (and I'm excited to devour every time I visit) is coffee orange. Everything about this combination makes sense: the bitter, chocolatey notes of coffee combined with the bright, acidic notes of orange. This is probably why Malai's Orange Fennel and Coffee Cardamom ice creams make my most favorite combination. Here, I feature this coffee orange duo in loaf form to make the ideal base for what would likely be my favorite ice cream cake ever. In fact, it turns into my perfect sundae on page 156.

MAKES 8–10 SERVINGS

½ cup unsalted butter, plus more for the pan

2 cups all-purpose flour, plus more for the pan

1 teaspoon baking powder

½ teaspoon baking soda

1 teaspoon salt

1 tablespoon instant espresso powder

1¾ cups packed light brown sugar

¾ cup plain whole-milk yogurt

Grated zest of 2 oranges

1. Preheat the oven to 350°F. Butter the bottom and sides of a 9 x 5-inch loaf pan, then dust with flour, tapping out the excess.

2. In a medium bowl, whisk together the flour, baking powder, baking soda, salt, and espresso powder.

3. In a medium saucepan, melt the butter over medium heat. Once the butter is melted, remove the pan from the heat and whisk in the sugar, yogurt, and orange zest until the sugar dissolves and all the ingredients are well blended. Using a rubber spatula, fold in the flour mixture until no dry ingredient streaks remain.

4. Pour the batter into the prepared pan. Bake the cake until the top is browned and a toothpick inserted into the center comes out clean, 30–40 minutes.

5. Let cool completely in the pan on a wire rack, then turn out of the pan to serve.

Orange Spiced Nankathai

Every few trips to India, we visit family in Surat, and every time we go, we get requests from our family in Ahmedabad—the city where my parents grew up—to be sure to bring back nankathai for them. Surat is known for its nankathai, which is a shortbread-like cookie made with semolina that is slightly sweet, rich, and perfect for dunking into a hot beverage. When I was developing a menu for Malai, I knew that nankathai would have to be included. To layer in more flavor, I added some salt, a bit more sugar, some spices, and cacao nibs for extra crunch. But I kept it true to the traditional recipe by using ghee and semolina.

MAKES 48 COOKIES

4 cups all-purpose flour

1¾ cups confectioners' sugar

½ cup coarse semolina flour

½ teaspoon baking soda

2 teaspoons salt

2 teaspoons chai masala (preferably Malai Chai Masala; see Malai Fun Fact, page 38)

1¾ cups ghee, at room temperature

Grated zest of 2 oranges

1 cup cacao nibs

1 Position 2 racks in the center of the oven and preheat the oven to 350°F. Line 2 sheet pans with parchment paper.

2 In a large bowl, whisk together the all-purpose flour, sugar, semolina flour, baking soda, salt, and chai masala. Using a rubber spatula, work the ghee and orange zest into the flour mixture until fully incorporated and a homogeneous dough forms. It will be sticky and moist. Add the cacao nibs and mix to distribute evenly.

3 Scoop up a spoonful of the dough, roll it between your palms into a 1-inch ball, flatten slightly, and place on a prepared sheet pan. Repeat with the remaining dough, spacing the cookies about ½ inch apart on the pans.

4 Bake the cookies, switching the pans between the racks and rotating the pans back to front about halfway through baking, until golden brown, about 13 minutes. Transfer to wire racks and let cool completely before serving.

Confetti Shortbread

Candied fennel seeds are souped-up sprinkles. They are colorful, just as sprinkles are, but they also have a really satisfying crunch and deliver the most welcoming punch of soft licorice flavor. They are excellent palate cleansers and digestives as well. Add them to a baked good and you get all the visual wow of rainbow sprinkles plus everything else. They're a pantry must-have, and here they dress up classic shortbread cookies.

MAKES 10–12 COOKIES

1 cup unsalted butter, at room temperature

⅔ cup confectioners' sugar

¼ teaspoon salt

2 cups all-purpose flour

½ cup candied fennel seeds

❶ Preheat the oven to 375°F. Line the bottom and sides of an 8-inch square baking pan with parchment paper, allowing the parchment to extend about 2 inches beyond the rim on two sides.

❷ In a large bowl, using a wooden spoon, mix together the butter, sugar, and salt until well blended. Add the flour and mix just until no white streaks remain. Add the fennel seeds and mix to distribute evenly.

❸ Transfer the dough to the prepared baking pan and press down evenly. Bake until the edges are lightly browned, about 20 minutes. Let the shortbread cool in the pan on a wire rack for 5 minutes. Using a sharp knife, score the warm shortbread into 10–12 pieces (I usually do diamonds), then let cool for about 20 minutes.

❹ Using the overhanging parchment, lift out the shortbread and place on a cutting board. Using the knife and your scored lines, cut into cookies. Transfer the cookies to the wire rack and let cool completely before serving.

Granola Chocolate Chip Cookies

When I was growing up, these were the only cookies that my mom would ever bake. She found a recipe on the back of the box of her favorite cereal and would make them for me and my sister when the time was right. It wasn't often, and it was always random, but what I remember most is coming home and smelling the nutty granola and chocolate and just *knowing* that there was a treat waiting for me. It was a no-brainer to eat them with Malai's ice creams. I changed up the cookie recipe to make them ice-cream-sandwich friendly: I substituted a bit of oil for some of the butter and included some ground fennel. Slight modifications, but they bring the same amount of joy.

MAKES 24 COOKIES

2 cups all-purpose flour

1 teaspoon baking soda

1 teaspoon salt

1 teaspoon ground fennel (see Pooja's Tip, page 168)

½ cup unsalted butter, at room temperature

¼ cup neutral oil, such as canola or sunflower

½ cup granulated cane sugar

½ cup packed light brown sugar

2 flax eggs (see Pooja's Tip)

1 teaspoon pure vanilla extract

1½ cups Magical Indian Granola (page 206) or your favorite granola

2 cups semisweet chocolate chips

1 pint Orange Fennel Ice Cream (page 45) or Ginger Root Ice Cream (page 35)

❶ Position 2 racks in the center of the oven and preheat the oven to 350°F. Line 2 sheet pans with parchment paper.

❷ In a medium bowl, whisk together the flour, baking soda, salt, and fennel.

❸ In a large bowl, using an electric mixer, beat together the butter and oil on medium speed until blended, about 1 minute. Add the granulated and brown sugars and beat until fluffy, about 2 minutes. Add the flax eggs and vanilla and beat until incorporated. Using a rubber spatula, fold in the flour mixture until mostly incorporated. Add the granola and chocolate chips and fold in until evenly distributed and no streaks of the flour mixture remain.

❹ Scoop out a tablespoon of the dough, roll it into a ball between your palms, and then flatten into a disk about 1 inch thick. Place the cookie on a prepared sheet pan. Repeat with the remaining dough, spacing the cookies about 2 inches apart on the pans.

❺ Bake the cookies, switching the pans between the racks and rotating the pans back to front about halfway through baking, until light golden brown, 12–15 minutes. Transfer the cookies to a wire rack and let cool completely. Repeat with the remaining dough, allowing the pans to cool before adding more cookies to them. To turn these into an ice cream sandwich, place a scoop of the ice cream between two cooled cookies and enjoy immediately.

POOJA'S TIP

To make the flax eggs, in a small bowl, combine 2 tablespoons ground flaxseeds (flaxseed meal) and 6 tablespoons water and let sit for 5 minutes.

Cardamom Doughnut Holes

I'm a big, big fan of eating hot and cold together. Biting into something steamy and then immediately cooling it off with frozen creaminess—there is nothing better. So this is my ideal dessert: fresh, hot doughnut holes paired with cool ice cream. It's a quick and easy recipe that tastes like a five-star dessert. The doughnut holes get an extra sparkle from a quick roll in cardamom sugar.

MAKES 35–40 DOUGHNUT HOLES

Neutral oil, such as grapeseed, for frying

½ cup plus 3 tablespoons granulated cane sugar

1 teaspoon ground cardamom

1¼ teaspoons salt

2 cups all-purpose flour

1½ tablespoons baking powder

1 cup whole milk

¼ cup plain whole-milk yogurt

4 tablespoons unsalted butter, melted and cooled slightly

Masala Chai Ice Cream (page 38), for serving

1 Place a wire rack on a sheet pan. Pour oil to a depth of 1 inch into a large, deep sauté pan or wide, shallow pot and heat over medium heat to 350°F.

2 While the oil is heating, in a small bowl, stir together ½ cup of the sugar, the cardamom, and ¼ teaspoon of the salt. Set aside.

3 In a large bowl, whisk together the flour, baking powder, the remaining 3 tablespoons sugar, and the remaining 1 teaspoon salt. In a medium bowl, whisk together the milk, yogurt, and butter until blended. Pour the milk mixture into the flour mixture and stir to form a thick, smooth batter.

4 When the oil is ready, using a 1-inch cookie scoop, drop balls of the batter into the hot oil, frying about 4 balls in each batch. The doughnut holes will expand to about 1½ inches, so be careful not to crowd the pan. Fry the doughnut holes on the first side for 2–3 minutes, then flip them over and fry for another 2 minutes. The balls will turn a deep brown on the outside, and that's fine. It is important to fry them until the center is cooked through.

5 Using a slotted spoon, transfer the doughnut holes to the wire rack to drain briefly, then roll in the cardamom sugar, coating them on all sides. Repeat with the remaining batter.

6 Serve the doughnut holes immediately with a scoop of ice cream alongside.

Cumin & Ajwain Biscuits

I first had this sweet-savory biscuit at a hotel in Bombay. The taste was so unexpected—the savory notes of the fruity cumin and peppery ajwain with the sugary bite of a shortbread cookie—and so delicious. The hotel was kind enough to give me the recipe, which I've played with since. These biscuits are incredible with a cup of chai, as part of a cheese board and, of course, with a scoop of ice cream. If you can't find ajwain seeds, caraway seeds are a great substitute.

MAKES 24 BISCUITS

2½ cups all-purpose flour, plus more for dusting

1½ teaspoons salt

2 teaspoons ground cinnamon

2 teaspoons cumin seeds

2 teaspoons ajwain or caraway seeds

1½ cups butter, at room temperature

½ cup confectioners' sugar

1 flax egg (see Pooja's Tip)

1 In a medium bowl, whisk together the flour, salt, cinnamon, cumin seeds, and ajwain seeds.

2 In a large bowl, using an electric mixer, beat together the butter and sugar on medium speed until light in color, 3–4 minutes. Add the flax egg and beat until fully incorporated. Using a rubber spatula, slowly fold the flour mixture into the butter mixture, mixing well. Gather the dough into a ball, wrap in plastic wrap, and refrigerate for 1 hour.

3 Preheat the oven to 350°F. Line a sheet pan with parchment paper.

4 On a lightly floured work surface, roll out the chilled dough ⅛–¼ inch thick. Using a 2-inch round biscuit cutter, cut out as many rounds as possible and place them on the prepared sheet pan, spacing them about ½ inch apart. Gather up and press together the dough scraps, roll out the dough, cut out as many rounds as possible, and add to the sheet pan.

5 Bake the biscuits until lightly golden on the edges, about 15 minutes. Transfer to a wire rack and let cool completely before serving.

POOJA'S TIP

To make the flax egg, in a small bowl, combine 1 tablespoon ground flaxseeds (flaxseed meal) and 3 tablespoons water and let sit for 5 minutes.

Jaggery Nutmeg Palmiers

My love affair with palmiers began at a young age. My dad often went to New York City on business and would always bring back treats from our favorite bakery. His bag would be filled with croissants, Danish pastries, and palmiers. As a sugar lover, I would always be searching for the palmiers. The crunch of the pastry with the small granules of sugar was so satisfying and irresistibly sweet. These have a bit more depth, as they call for jaggery instead of sugar and include a bit of nutmeg for warmth. Other than that, they're just as I remember those New York palmiers. Be sure to serve them with ice cream.

MAKES 40–45 COOKIES

1 cup powdered jaggery
(see Pooja's Tip, page 41)

¼ teaspoon salt

1 sheet puff pastry, about
17.3 ounces, thawed according
to package directions

½ teaspoon ground nutmeg

1 Position 2 racks in the center of the oven and preheat the oven to 450°F. Line 2 sheet pans with parchment paper.

2 In a small bowl, stir together ½ cup of the jaggery and the salt, mixing well. Pour it onto a clean work surface and spread evenly. Unfold the puff pastry sheet directly on the jaggery mixture.

3 In the same small bowl, stir together the remaining ½ cup jaggery and the nutmeg, mixing well. Spread it on the puff pastry, covering the pastry completely. It should be a thick, even coating. With a rolling pin, lightly roll the dough until it is a 13-inch square and the sugar is pressed into the puff pastry on the top and bottom.

4 Fold the left and right sides of the square toward the center so they reach halfway to the middle. Fold them toward the center again so the two folds meet exactly at the center of the dough. Then fold one half over the other half as if closing a book. You will have six layers. Slice the layered dough crosswise into ⅜-inch-thick slices. Place the slices, cut side up, on the prepared sheet pans, spacing them about 1 inch apart.

5 Bake the cookies until caramelized and browned on the bottom, about 7 minutes. Then, using a spatula, turn them over, return the pans to the oven, switching them between the racks and rotating them back to front, and bake until caramelized and browned on the second side, about 4 minutes longer. Transfer the cookies to wire racks and let cool completely before serving.

Toppings & Sauces

Chocolate Cardamom Sauce

I will unequivocally say that the most delicious fast-food dessert is a McDonald's hot fudge sundae. Rich, warm, gooey, decadent chocolate sauce cascading over a cool bowl of melting ice cream. Come on! There is nothing better. My sister (who also will never pass up this fast-food dessert) and I have discussed this at length—the thing that makes this over-the-top delicious is its satisfying *thickness*.

That's what I've recreated here—except, dare I say, better. It's all the qualities of the fast-food sundae sauce but with the added nuance and depth of cardamom. This spooned over a scoop of Orange Fennel Ice Cream (page 45) is a dessert that McD's cannot beat.

MAKES ABOUT 1 CUP

½ cup unsweetened natural cocoa powder

1 cup granulated cane sugar

½ teaspoon salt

½ cup water

1 teaspoon ground cardamom

1 In a small saucepan, whisk together the cocoa powder, sugar, and salt. Pour in the water, stir to mix, and bring to a boil over medium heat, stirring constantly and scraping down the sides of the pan with a rubber spatula for an even texture. Reduce the heat to a simmer and continue stirring and scraping for about 30 more seconds. Stir in the cardamom, remove from the heat, and let cool for about 10 minutes.

2 Use immediately, or let cool to room temperature and store in an airtight container in the refrigerator for up to 2 weeks.

Cherry Rose Syrup

When it comes to dressing up ice cream, the decadent sauces are always at the top of everyone's list: hot fudge, caramel, toffee, peanut butter, and more. I love them, too, and this cookbook has recipes for some of them. But sometimes we all want a fresh punch of something bright and acidic. This rose-scented cherry syrup is tart and intense and has a faint floral note from the addition of rose water. It can definitely rival a lush and creamy sauce.

MAKES ABOUT 2 CUPS

4 cups fresh or frozen cherries (if using fresh, be sure they are pitted)

½ cup honey

½ cup agave nectar

1¼ teaspoons salt

2 tablespoons rose water

1 In a saucepan, combine the cherries, honey, agave nectar, and salt over medium heat and bring to a simmer, stirring occasionally. Cook, stirring often, until the mixture reduces and is slightly thickened, about 5 minutes. Remove from the heat and let cool to room temperature.

2 Transfer the cooled mixture to a blender and process until smooth, about 2 minutes. Transfer to a bowl and stir in the rose water. Use immediately, or transfer to an airtight container and store in the refrigerator for up to 3 days.

Spicy Peanut Butter Sauce

There is something about peanut butter. The salty, creamy nuttiness is something that cannot be beat and is so satiating. Because I love a peanut butter sauce on my ice cream, I created this one for Malai. It's silky and smooth and pairs well with the warming, spicy notes of the garam masala. The funny thing is, we never actually sold this peanut butter sauce at Malai. Fortunately, it's always at your disposal here.

MAKES ABOUT 2 CUPS

½ cup heavy cream

½ cup water

½ cup packed light brown sugar

½ cup granulated cane sugar

1 cup creamy natural peanut butter

¾ teaspoon pure vanilla extract

2 teaspoons garam masala (see Pooja's Tip)

1 teaspoon salt

❶ In a saucepan, combine the cream, water, brown and granulated sugars, peanut butter, vanilla, garam masala, and salt and whisk to mix well. Place over medium heat and heat, stirring occasionally, until the mixture comes to a boil, about 5 minutes.

❷ Remove from the heat and let cool to room temperature. Use immediately, or transfer to an airtight container and store in the refrigerator for up to 3 days.

POOJA'S TIP
Garam masalas tend to differ from brand to brand. Look for a garam masala that contains a lot of warming spices—cinnamon, star anise, and cloves. My favorite brand for my dessert recipes (and the one that we use at Malai) is Cardoz Legacy.

Jaggery Fennel Caramel Sauce

Buttery and rich, this caramel sauce is taken to the next level with the bold, sweet flavors of ground fennel. I recommend toasting and grinding whole fennel seeds for the brightest, freshest flavor. While brown sugar can be used here, I encourage you to seek out jaggery for its more subtle sweetness.

MAKES ABOUT 1 CUP

½ cup unsalted butter

½ cup heavy cream

½ cup jaggery (powdered or shaved from a block; see Pooja's Tip, page 41) or packed light brown sugar

½ teaspoon salt

¾ teaspoon ground fennel (see Pooja's Tip, page 168)

❶ In a small saucepan, combine the butter, cream, jaggery, and salt over medium heat and heat, stirring constantly with a rubber spatula, until the mixture begins to boil. Reduce the heat to a simmer and cook, continuing to stir and scrape down the sides, until the mixture thickens and becomes golden brown, 5–7 minutes. Remove from the heat, stir in the fennel, and let cool for about 10 minutes.

❷ Use immediately, or let cool to room temperature and store in an airtight container in the refrigerator for up to 1 week.

Cone Crunch

This topping, the most popular at Malai, was created by chance. We received a box of cones, and an entire sleeve arrived crushed. To save the crushed cones, we turned them into a topping. What we came up with is the perfect amount of crunch, sweetness, and pop that you need for any ice cream—and especially great for those that want a cone but find it too messy!

MAKES ABOUT 2 CUPS

½ cup unsalted butter

2¼ teaspoons honey

½ teaspoon salt

3 cups crushed waffle cones (the pieces should be about ½–1 inch in size)

¼ cup non-fat milk powder

¼ cup granulated cane sugar

❶ Preheat the oven to 300°F. Line a sheet pan with parchment paper.

❷ In a small saucepan, combine the butter, honey, and salt over medium-low heat and heat, stirring, until the butter and honey have melted and the mixture is smooth, about 5 minutes. Remove from the heat.

❸ In a large bowl, stir together the crushed cones, milk powder, and sugar, mixing well. Pour the warm butter mixture over the cone mixture and, using a rubber spatula, toss until all the cone pieces are evenly coated.

❹ Transfer the mixture to the prepared sheet pan and spread in an even layer. Bake for 7 minutes. Remove from the oven and toss the mixture to ensure even baking. Then return the pan to the oven and continue to bake the cone mixture until golden and toasty, about 7 minutes longer.

❺ Remove from the oven and let cool completely before using. Store in an airtight container at room temperature for up to 1 week.

Spiced Honey

This topping—great on ice cream, of course, but also a delight on cakes, cheese, and crackers—is so delicious you'll be wondering why it isn't a staple in your pantry. It should be, and this is your cue to make it so.

MAKES ABOUT 2 CUPS

2 cups honey

1 teaspoon ground cinnamon

½ teaspoon ground cardamom

½ teaspoon ground ginger

½ teaspoon freshly grated nutmeg

¼ teaspoon kosher salt

⅛ teaspoon ground cloves

⅛ teaspoon ground black pepper

2 teaspoons vanilla bean paste

❶ In a small saucepan, combine the honey, cinnamon, cardamom, ginger, nutmeg, salt, cloves, and pepper over low heat and heat, stirring constantly and gently, until the honey and spices are well blended and the mixture is heated through, about 10 minutes.

❷ Remove from the heat and stir in the vanilla paste, then let cool in the pan. Serve warm or at room temperature. Store in an airtight container at room temperature.

Peanut Chikki

I spent as many December holiday breaks in India as I did summers. The summers had glorious monsoon rains, all the mangoes I could dream of, and going out for ice golas every night after dinner. But the winters were also special. There were street vendors who served roasted white sweet potatoes, custard apples were available at fruit stands, and the Uttarayan festival was held. Uttarayan takes place every January in Gujarat and marks the end of the winter season. It's celebrated by everyone going out on rooftops and flying kites and snacking all day long. All you see in the sky are countless colorful diamonds, each one a kite, and all you see next to you is peanut chikki, the unofficial snack of Uttarayan. This brittle, made with jaggery, is the perfect snack to keep energies up for an all-day festival and provides just the right amount of sweetness. We may not have a big kite festival here in New York, but at least we can have the chikki.

MAKES ABOUT 3 CUPS

Nonstick cooking spray, for the pan

2¼ cups jaggery (shaved from a block; see Pooja's Tip, page 41)

¼ cup ghee

1 tablespoon salt

4 cups skinless raw peanuts, very finely chopped

❶ Line a sheet pan with parchment paper. Spray the parchment with cooking spray. Tear off an equal-size sheet of parchment and spray it on one side with cooking spray. Set both the pan and the parchment aside.

❷ In a saucepan, combine the jaggery, ghee, and salt. Place over medium-high heat and whisk the mixture constantly until it registers 300°F on an instant-read thermometer. Moving quickly, stir in the peanuts and then carefully transfer the mixture to the prepared sheet pan. Lay the second parchment sheet, cooking spray side down, over the peanuts. Using a rolling pin and working swiftly and carefully, spread the peanut mixture evenly over the sheet pan. The mixture is very hot and will harden quickly.

❸ Set the pan aside to cool. Remove the top sheet of parchment. Once the chikki has cooled, lift it off the pan and break or chop it into pieces. Enjoy immediately, or store in an airtight container at room temperature for up to 2 weeks.

POOJA'S TIP

Once the chikki has cooled, freeze it and then make Magic Shell (page 200). Drizzle the frozen chikki pieces with the Magic Shell to create a very satisfying chocolate-covered chikki.

Plum Sauce

This plum sauce almost never happened. Years ago, we were visiting my aunt's family in India, and they served a delicious welcome drink of plum juice—a sweet and salty, slightly spiced juice that was very refreshing. I was obsessed. I asked my aunt's family for the recipe, and my mom and I tried it at home. We made it, tasted it, and it was an exact replica. It needed to be on the heat for just a few minutes longer and it would be ready. So we left it on the stove and walked away—and forgot about it. The plum juice reduced to a thick, smooth sauce that was definitely undrinkable. Instead, we poured it over vanilla ice cream, and it was one of the best sauces we had ever had. To this day, we make this recipe every year—as a sauce!

MAKES ABOUT 1 CUP

8–9 ripe but firm black plums, halved and pitted

½–¾ cup water

1½ cups granulated cane sugar

2 teaspoons salt

2 teaspoons jiralu powder (see Pooja's Tip)

1. In a medium saucepan, combine the plums and ½ cup of the water over medium heat and bring to a boil. Boil the plums, stirring often and adding a little more water if the pan seems too dry, until they are fork-tender and falling apart, 6–8 minutes.

2. Remove from the heat and let cool slightly. Transfer the plums and any liquid to a blender and blend until a smooth purée forms. Strain the purée through a fine-mesh sieve to remove the skins.

3. Return the purée to the pan. If the purée seems too thick like applesauce, add a little more water. Place the pan over medium heat and stir in the sugar, salt, and jiralu powder. Bring the mixture to a rolling boil, stirring occasionally, and boil for about 1 minute, then reduce the heat to low.

4. Remove from the heat and let cool to room temperature. Transfer to an airtight container and refrigerate until cold before serving. The sauce will keep for up to 1 week.

POOJA'S TIP

Jiralu is a combination of salt, ground cumin, ground ginger, chili powder, and ground turmeric. It is commonly available at Indian grocery stores, but you can create your own blend by mixing 1 teaspoon ground cumin, ½ teaspoon ground allspice, ½ teaspoon ground ginger, and ½ teaspoon salt. You can also flavor this sauce however you please. For instance, ground cinnamon would be delicious here, and maybe a pinch of ground cardamom.

Magic Shell

Can we all agree that a magic shell on top of a scoop of ice cream is always exciting? Watching a hot liquid poured over a creamy scoop of cold ice cream turn into a hard, solid topping is just like . . . science class! Because both chocolate and coconut oil can exist in liquid and solid states, this is an especially easy and natural way to make a chocolate shell. And you can spice it up to take it to the next level: ground cardamom with a chocolate shell, ground fennel seeds with a butterscotch shell, rose water with a white chocolate shell. Experiment with your favorite flavors and taste the magic.

**MAKES ENOUGH
FOR 8–10 SCOOPS
OF ICE CREAM**

3 tablespoons coconut oil

1 cup chocolate chips

1 teaspoon ground cardamom

❶ In the top of a double boiler, combine the coconut oil and chocolate chips. Place over (not touching) simmering water in the lower pan and heat, stirring occasionally, just until the chocolate and oil have melted and the mixture is smooth. (You can also melt the mixture in a microwave using 30-second bursts, stirring after each burst.) Remove from the heat and stir in the cardamom. Set the sauce aside for 10 minutes to cool slightly before using.

❷ To use, drizzle over a scoop of ice cream, add any extra toppings (such as sprinkles, nuts, and edible flowers), let sit for 15 seconds to harden, and then enjoy. Store any leftover sauce in an airtight container in the refrigerator for up to 1 week. When ready to use, gently reheat in a double boiler or in the microwave to bring back the smooth consistency.

POOJA'S TIP

Other flavor options include white chocolate chips with 1½ teaspoons rose water, butterscotch chips with 1½ teaspoons ground toasted fennel seeds, or peanut butter chips with ¼ teaspoon cayenne pepper.

Blueberry Cardamom Sauce

This is likely to become your go-to fruit sauce. It's unbelievably easy to put together, and it goes well on everything: certainly ice cream but also pancakes, oatmeal, waffles, your fingers, a shoe. Bonus: it's equally delicious with fresh and frozen berries so you can have it all year round. Now that you have it, use it and never let it leave your repertoire.

MAKES ABOUT 2 CUPS

6 cups blueberries

2 cups plus 1 tablespoon water

1 cup granulated cane sugar

1 tablespoon ground cardamom

1 tablespoon fresh lemon juice

1 teaspoon cornstarch

1 In a wide, shallow pan, combine the blueberries, 2 cups of the water, the sugar, cardamom, and lemon juice and bring to a boil over medium heat, stirring occasionally. While the berry mixture heats, in a small bowl, stir together the cornstarch and the remaining 1 tablespoon water to make a slurry.

2 When the berry mixture reaches a boil, stir in the slurry, bring the mixture back to a boil, and boil for about 1 minute. Reduce the heat to a simmer and cook, stirring occasionally, until the sauce thickens, about 5 minutes longer.

3 Remove from the heat and let cool for a few minutes before spooning over ice cream. Or let cool completely, transfer to an airtight container, and store in the refrigerator for up to 1 week.

Spiced Whipped Cream

Did someone ask for a spiced cloud? If the answer is yes, this whipped topping is all you need. It's a welcome addition to any ice cream (cream on cream? yes!) and can also add a richness to fruity and floral sorbets. Plus, you can make it vegan by substituting coconut cream for the heavy cream.

MAKES ABOUT 2 CUPS

---

1 cup heavy cream

1 tablespoon granulated cane sugar

2 teaspoons ground spice of choice (such as cinnamon, cardamom, nutmeg, or even bloomed saffron)

Pinch of salt

❶ In a bowl, beat the cream until soft peaks form, about 4 minutes with a hand mixer, or 5–6 minutes by hand with a whisk. Sprinkle the sugar, spice, and salt on top and beat for 30 more seconds to mix thoroughly. Use immediately.

Spiced Muddy Buddies

I have never been impressed with the name of this nostalgic childhood treat—most commonly known as *muddy* buddies or often called *puppy* chow. Once I actually got past the name, I gave these bites a try and was able to understand the hype. On the surface, their popularity defies all logic—their name is unappealing, their appearance is equally so. But the taste is pure joy and nostalgia. And for that reason alone, you should make these muddy, puppy chow buddies. There is a sprinkling of chai masala in this version, which adds to the depth of the treat, but you can adjust the type and quantity to your liking.

MAKES ABOUT 6 CUPS

9 cups Rice Chex

1 cup dark chocolate chips

⅓ cup creamy natural peanut butter

⅓ cup store-bought Biscoff cookie butter

4 tablespoons unsalted butter

1 tablespoon chai masala (see Pooja's Tip, page 38)

1 teaspoon salt

1 teaspoon pure vanilla extract

1½ cups confectioners' sugar

❶ Put the cereal into a large bowl. Set aside.

❷ In a medium microwave-safe bowl, combine the chocolate chips, peanut butter, cookie butter, and unsalted butter and microwave in 30-second bursts, stirring after each burst, until everything has melted and the mixture is smooth. Add the chai masala, salt, and vanilla to the chocolate mixture and stir to mix well.

❸ Using a rubber spatula and stirring constantly to make sure the cereal does not break up, mix the chocolate mixture into the cereal until the cereal is evenly coated.

❹ Divide the cereal mixture evenly between two 1-gallon ziplock bags. Add ¾ cup of the sugar to each bag. Press the air out of the bags, seal closed, and shake the bags until the cereal mixture is coated with the sugar.

❺ Line 2 sheet pans with waxed paper. Pour each bag of cereal out onto a prepared sheet pan, spreading it in an even layer. Let sit until the cereal mixture has cooled completely and the chocolate has hardened before serving. Store in an airtight container at room temperature for up to 1 week.

Magical Indian Granola

During part of my college study-abroad semester in Argentina, a friend and I got an apartment in Buenos Aires. During our stay, my mom would often send me care packages with all my favorite foods. In one of those packages, she included homemade granola from a recipe that we found online, tweaked to our taste, and had been making for years. My roommate looked into the box, grabbed the bag of granola, and shoveled some into his mouth. His eyes widened, and the first thing he said was, "This is magical Indian granola!" Turns out that there isn't anything Indian about it (though you can change up the spices; see Pooja's Tip), but it is most definitely magical. And it's a delight sprinkled over ice cream.

MAKES ABOUT 6 CUPS

4 cups old-fashioned rolled oats

3 cups any combination of nuts and dried fruits (see Pooja's Tip)

2 teaspoons ground cinnamon (see Pooja's Tip)

½ teaspoon salt

¼ cup neutral oil, such as sunflower or canola

¼ cup honey

¼ cup grade A maple syrup

1 teaspoon pure vanilla extract

❶ Preheat the oven to 300°F. Line a sheet pan with parchment paper.

❷ In a large bowl, combine the oats, nuts and fruits, cinnamon, and salt and stir to mix. In a medium bowl, whisk together the oil, honey, maple syrup, and vanilla. Pour the oil mixture over the oats mixture and mix until the oats mixture is evenly coated.

❸ Pour the mixture out onto the prepared sheet pan and spread in an even layer. Bake the granola, stirring every 15 minutes to ensure even baking, until dry, 1 to 1¼ hours. Let cool completely on the pan, then transfer to an airtight container and store at room temperature for up to 2 weeks.

POOJA'S TIP

My favorite combination of nuts and dried fruits for this recipe is 1 cup slivered almonds, 1 cup chopped pecans, and 1 cup unsweetened shredded dried coconut. You can swap out the cinnamon for another warming spice, such as cardamom or nutmeg, or use a mixture of all.

Apple Butter Chutney

When my parents' generation first came to the United States, there were many Indian ingredients that were not readily available here. So they had to develop hacks with commonly found foods in American grocery stores. One of the most common hacks was to use apple butter as a base for date tamarind chutney, a popular everyday condiment. It has the same sweetness and texture as the chutney, and it's already spiced—it just needed to be doctored up a bit. My mom told me about this hack in case I was ever craving chutney and was pressed for time to make the real thing. Turns out that it's also a great topping for a scoop of ice cream.

MAKES ABOUT 1 CUP

1 cup apple butter

1 teaspoon ground coriander

1 teaspoon ground cumin

½ teaspoon ground cinnamon

¼ teaspoon ground cloves

1 teaspoon Kashmiri red chili powder

¼ teaspoon salt

¼ cup water

1 tablespoon fresh lemon juice

❶ In a small bowl, stir together the apple butter, coriander, cumin, cinnamon, cloves, chili powder, and salt, mixing well. Stir in the water and lemon juice. Transfer the mixture to a small saucepan, place over medium heat, and heat, stirring occasionally, until warmed through and the flavors have melded, about 5 minutes.

❷ Remove from the heat and let cool completely. Use immediately, or transfer to an airtight container and store in the refrigerator for up to 1 week.

Vanilla & Cardamom Almond Clusters

To my mind, what makes a great ice cream topping is that it's something you may also want to snack on by itself. This is one of those great toppings—yes, it's great on top of a scoop—but these clusters are also superior as a midafternoon (or midnight) treat. Feel free to experiment with the type of extract and the spice.

MAKES ABOUT 1½ CUPS

Nonstick cooking spray, for the pan

1 flax egg (see Pooja's Tip, page 180)

1 teaspoon pure vanilla extract

2 cups whole raw almonds

⅔ cup granulated cane sugar

¼ teaspoon salt

½ teaspoon ground cardamom

❶ Preheat the oven to 300°F. Spray a sheet pan with cooking spray.

❷ In a medium bowl, stir together the flax egg and vanilla, mixing well. Add the almonds and stir to coat. In a small bowl, stir together the sugar, salt, and cardamom, mixing well. Add the sugar mixture to the almonds and stir and toss to coat the almonds evenly.

❸ Pour the almonds onto the prepared sheet pan and spread in a single layer. Bake the almonds until golden, about 20 minutes.

❹ Remove the pan from oven and let the almonds cool on the baking sheet. Let cool completely and then break into clusters. Let cool completely and then break into clusters. Store in an airtight container at room temperature for up to 1 week.

ACKNOWLEDGMENTS

I've never written a cookbook before. What an experience! These are the people who guided me, supported me, encouraged me, and cheered me on throughout this process.

First and foremost, my deepest gratitude to my family. You supported me and Malai before the ice cream even existed, and I would not have been able to do any of it without you. You have been game for cookbook shoots, cookbook inspiration, and cookbook taste testing—nothing was off-limits. You are always, without question or hesitation, there for me, and I can truly ask for nothing more.

A huge shout-out to the Malai team! Thank you to Malai's director of brand, Kim. You took on every single aspect of this project—even things you had never done before—to ensure its success. I could not have done this without you. Thank you also to Malai's production lead, Jae. You tested every single recipe in this book and kindly gave suggestions where needed. And thank you to the rest of Malai's marketing and design team, Bella, Evelyn, and Nellie, for all

your hard work. Lastly, thank you to Ben, Malai's director of operations, who kept the business side of the company going while we all focused on the book. Putting together this cookbook, more than anything else I have done in recent memory, truly embodied the "it takes a village" mentality, and I'm so grateful for the supportive Malai village we have built. It is an honor to work together every day.

Thank you to my agent, Jonah, for guiding me through this process with kindness and patience and for loving Malai so much. You started this race with me, and I'm happy to be crossing the finish line together.

Thank you to my talented photo team: Morgan, Judy, Maeve, and Zach. You all showed me that I was in the best hands possible during the biggest photoshoot I have ever done. Just look at the photography in this book! I couldn't be prouder.

Morgan, you've been Malai's photographer from the very beginning, and you were the first person to tell me that I should write a cookbook. You helped create Malai's brand aesthetic and have embodied it ever since. There is no one else I would have trusted with this project, and I am so proud of the work we have created together—in this book and throughout the years.

Thank you to the hardworking team at Weldon Owen, who welcomed me with open arms, and a special note of gratitude to my editor, Amy.

Thank you to my best friends, who have been beyond supportive throughout this entire journey.

You have all been (individually) asking for the very first copy of this cookbook, and your time has arrived!

To my Risu, who keeps my world going round and round. Nothing makes me happier than knowing that Malai is your most favorite. I can't wait to cook our way through this book together.

Finally, thank you to all of Malai's customers and supporters. You have been encouraging me to write a cookbook for years, all stemming from your love of Malai. I hope that this recipe collection is all that you wanted and more. None of this would exist without you, and for that, **I am grateful.**

INDEX

ABOUT THE AUTHOR

Pooja Bavishi is the founder and CEO of Malai, an acclaimed New York–based ice cream company and scoop shop specializing in innovative flavors infused with traditional South Asian ingredients. Inspired by the spices of her childhood—ginger, rose petals, fennel, saffron, and cardamom—Pooja opened Malai in 2015 to offer a unique ice cream experience that blends her rich culinary heritage with everyone's favorite frozen dessert. The success of Malai soon led to other accomplishments. She won Food Network's *Chopped Sweets* competition in March 2020, was recognized as one of *Inc.* magazine's Female Founders 100 in October 2020, and was named a Tory Burch Foundation Fellow in 2018. Pooja holds a BA from the University of North Carolina at Chapel Hill, an MS from the London School of Economics, and an MBA from NYU's Stern School of Business.

PRAISE FOR *MALAI*

"Malai delightfully celebrates cultural traditions while also providing a new canvas for exploration for any skill level. The recipes are accessible, but the flavors are out of this world—a refreshing dessert guide that's sure to be a crowd-pleaser, if you're willing to share." **—Meena Harris, founder and CEO, Phenomenal Media**

"My neighborhood became decidedly more delicious the day Malai opened its doors. What appeared at first to be just another frozen treat shop has transformed and enchanted our little corner of Brooklyn in ways we could never have imagined, drawing ice cream fanatics from New York City and beyond for a taste of Pooja's enlightened, transporting creations. Now with the Malai cookbook, we can all get a glimpse of the magic she churns each day and learn to make her singular creations ourselves. Malai's ice cream is not just a joy to eat. It's a powerful connection to a broader world for flavor lovers of all ages!" **—Gail Simmons, food expert, TV host, and author of** *Bringing It Home*

"Pooja is the perfect guide for ice cream lovers looking to make frozen treats at home—which means this book is the perfect guide for everyone! She has grown Malai with such love and intention, and that love and intention overflow into her recipes. They represent the delicious, fabulous blend of her Indian roots and American upbringing—the best of both coming together seamlessly." **—Barkha Cardoz, founder of Cardoz Legacy and author of** *With Love & Masalas*

"When I think of my favorite ice cream shops, Malai is always at the top of my list. The way Pooja combines vibrant Indian-inspired flavors and spices is like nothing I've seen anywhere else. She is a singular creative, and I'm so happy to see her cookbook out in the world." **—Kerry Diamond, founder,** *Cherry Bombe*

"Pooja Bavishi shows us how ice cream can tell the story of who we are and where we come from. The Malai cookbook changes the way we think about ice cream—Pooja's flavor combinations are unmatched, layered with spices, bursting with color, and infused with the richness of her Indian American experience. A sweet triumph." **—Hetty Lui McKinnon, James Beard Award– winning cookbook author and food writer**

"Turn up the joy, the nostalgia, the color, the flavor in life in all things ice cream with my pal Pooja as your guide. These pages are an invitation to a drool-worthy, magical world of dessert that starts in India but stretches to every place your heart, imagination, and taste buds have traveled to or dreamed of going. Make sure you pack a bib and a spoon for the delicious journey." **—Christina Tosi, chef and founder, Milk Bar**

weldon**owen**

an imprint of Insight Editions
P.O. Box 3088
San Rafael, CA 94912
www.weldonowen.com

CEO Raoul Goff
VP Publisher Roger Shaw
Publishing Director Katie Killebrew
VP Creative Chrissy Kwasnik
Senior Editor Karyn Gerhard
Editorial Assistant Jon Ellis
Art Director & Designer Megan Sinead Bingham
Production Designer Jean Hwang
VP Manufacturing Alix Nicholaeff
Production Manager Joshua Smith
Sr Production Manager, Subsidiary Rights Lina s Palma-Temena

Editor Amy Marr
Photographer Morgan Ione Yeager
Food Stylist Judy Haubert
Prop Stylist Maeve Sheridan
Lighting Zach Felts

Weldon Owen would also like to thank Elizabeth Parson and Sharon Silva.
Special thanks to Bella DelMonico for designing the endpapers and
collaborating on the back cover.

ISBN: 979-8-88674-187-2

Manufactured in China by Insight Editions
10 9 8 7 6 5 4 3 2 1

ROOTS of PEACE   REPLANTED PAPER

Insight Editions, in association with Roots of Peace, will plant two trees for each tree
used in the manufacturing of this book. Roots of Peace is an internationally renowned
humanitarian organization dedicated to eradicating land mines worldwide and
converting war-torn lands into productive farms and wildlife habitats. Roots of Peace
will plant two million fruit and nut trees in Afghanistan and provide farmers there with
the skills and support necessary for sustainable land use.